Preventing Disruptive Behavior in Colleges

A Campus and Classroom Management Handbook for Higher Education

Howard Seeman

ROWMAN & LITTLEFIELD EDUCATION

A division of
ROWMAN & LITTLEFIELD PUBLISHERS, INC.
Lanham • Boulder • New York • Toronto • Plymouth, UK

Published by Rowman & Littlefield Education
A division of Rowman & Littlefield Publishers, Inc.
A wholly owned subsidiary of The Rowman & Littlefield Publishing Group, Inc.
4501 Forbes Boulevard, Suite 200, Lanham, Maryland 20706
http://www.rowmaneducation.com

Estover Road, Plymouth PL6 7PY, United Kingdom

British Library Cataloguing in Publication Information Available

Library of Congress Cataloging-in-Publication Data

Seeman, Howard.
   Preventing disruptive behavior in colleges : a campus and classroom management
handbook for higher education / Howard Seeman.
      p. cm.
   Includes bibliographical references and index.
   ISBN 978-1-60709-391-6 (cloth : alk. paper) — ISBN 978-1-60709-392-3 (pbk. : alk.
paper) — ISBN 978-1-60709-393-0 (electronic)
   1. Classroom management—United States. 2. College discipline—United States.
3. College students—United States—Psychology. I. Title.
LB3013.S444 2010
371.102'4—dc22   2009017243

Printed in the United States of America

Contents

PART III: THIS BOOK AS A HANDBOOK

Acknowledgments

I would first like to thank Professor Rosalyn Baxandall for thoroughly reading the manuscript, her excellent suggestions of needed revisions and additions, her review, and her emotional support in general that enabled me to work on this project.

I also want to thank Professors Ira Altman and Daniel J. Wiener for their editorial suggestions to the manuscript and for reviewing it; Professor Peter Stein for his suggestions and support; and all my dear friends, family, and Jaimelyn who bring great meaning, and therefore "motivation to do," to my life in general.

Introduction:
You Are Not Alone

A. Disruptive Behavior Has Been a Major Problem in Schools K–12
B. This Problem Is Now Spreading Into Colleges
C. Why Is This Happening?

A. DISRUPTIVE BEHAVIOR HAS BEEN A
MAJOR PROBLEM IN SCHOOLS K–12

In national surveys of the public's attitude toward K–12 education since 1974, disruptive classroom behaviors, "discipline problems," have been cited as a major problem. Concern about discipline consistently has been rated higher than concerns about drug abuse, poor curriculum, academic standards, and even lack of appropriate financial support.[1] In one survey, teachers throughout the state of New York cited "managing disruptive children" in classrooms as the most stressful problem in their professional lives; indeed, the problem was rated as the highest stress factor among these teachers, regardless of their age, type of school district, sex, marital status, or grade level.[2] Similar findings have also appeared in studies of Chicago teachers[3] and teachers in Great Britain.[4]

In response to the above problem, after conducting many workshops and delivering keynote speeches on this subject across the United States, in 1988 I wrote the first edition of the book *Preventing Classroom Discipline Problems* to prevent and handle disruptive behaviors especially in the junior and senior high schools where they were the most severe and prevalent. However, disruptive behavior continued to escalate: For example, in New York State in 1993, teachers reported a 91 percent increase in the use of profanity in the classroom and an 87 percent increase of student defiance of teachers.

So, in 1994 I wrote the second edition of this book to respond to this increasing problem, and also to address problems in grades K–6 as well— because the kinds and causes of disruptive behaviors in these lower grades were not only different, but often required a different approach. Then, in 2000, I wrote the third edition of this book, again to speak to a problem now erupting into violence and starting to endanger all schools and the teaching profession itself.

Each month approximately three percent of teachers and students in urban schools, and one to two percent in rural schools, are robbed or physically attacked. Nearly 17,000 students per month experience physical injuries serious enough to require medical attention; school and classroom disruptions lead to nearly two million suspensions per year.[5]

We lose potentially "good" teachers every year: Our nation is always in trouble with recruiting enough teachers; 50 percent quit the profession within five years. When asked why they left, the most frequent reason given is the stress around classroom disruptive behavior.[6]

Also, overseas in the United Kingdom, a

teachers' union survey suggests poor discipline in the classroom is a continuing problem. A survey for the Association of Teachers and Lecturers, UK, [indicates] 99% of teachers have dealt with disruptive pupils . . . and 71% have considered leaving the profession because of bad behavior in the classroom. . . . [Also,] 37% said they had suffered mental health problems as a result.[7]

I am proud to report that theaforementioned first edition of my book is now used successfully in over 400 school districts in the United States, coast to coast, and in over thirty-five countries. However, the problem of disruptive behavior continues to spread.

B. THIS PROBLEM IS NOW SPREADING INTO COLLEGES

I now find it necessary to offer help to teachers regarding disruptive behavior with college students, especially in the first few semesters of higher education. Bulletins, memos, websites, reports, workshops, college faculty meetings . . . are now discussing a growing frequency of disruptive behavior in college classrooms, especially in the undergraduate years.

Here are a few examples:

- Eric # ED204300: Crime and Disruptive Behavior. A Module of Instruction for Colleges of Education in the State of Louisiana. Bulletin No. 1560, 16 pages.
- One article from the *New York Times* is "Colleges Tightening Discipline as Disruptive Behavior Grows." Although there are no overall statistics yet on this problem in higher education, some college officials cite increasing instances of verbal abuse, physical threats, property damage and extreme conduct that is threatening and disruptive in college classrooms. They tell of students who . . . badger and hector instructors, interrupting class and creating scenes on campus.[8]
- On college campuses, the term "disruptive behavior" was most commonly associated with large-scale demonstrations and protests. There is, however, another form of misconduct on campus which is seldom reported by the media but which causes individual faculty members considerably more personal turmoil: disruptive behavior in the classroom. . . . The climate of higher education has changed over the past few decades, and faculty are now faced with serious issues of classroom behavior that were previously of little concern.[9]
- It is shown that increasingly immature, and even violent, behavior is a problem nationwide at both two-year and four-year colleges.[10]
- A recent survey examining student learning in the college classroom found disruptive student behavior to be a major learning inhibitor. Compounding this is the realization that most college faculty are ill prepared to handle this problem.

This result is hardly surprising. Incidents of disruptive behavior are becoming more common in college classrooms. What is surprising, however, is that disruptive behavior impacts the students just as much—if not more—than the professors. Many times students are the ones who are telling their fellow students to be quiet.[11] Colleges all over the country are not only issuing memos and administrative pamphlets to their faculty on the subject, but also holding faculty meetings and sometimes workshops to address the problem. For example:

27th ANNUAL CONF. ON THE FIRST YEAR COLLEGE
EXPERIENCE, FEB. 15, 2008

A-17 Preventing and Responding to Disruptive Behavior in the Classroom

Saturday, February 16, 2008, 1:00 p.m.–5:00 p.m.—$135

Limited to 50 participants

*W. Scott Lewis, Assistant Vice Provost for Judicial Affairs and Academic
Integrity—University of South Carolina*

Over the last ten years, there has been an increase in the number and severity of behavioral incidents in the classrooms and on campuses. More and
more, it is incumbent upon instructors to intervene in the classroom to address
behaviors that can interfere with teaching and learning. Using a combina-
tion of lecture and case studies taken from actual incidents, this workshop
will provide attendees with tools to appropriately address these behaviors.
Participants will be provided with skills to prevent disruptive behaviors, and
to react to them, and tips on how to enhance their own campus procedures to
address those behaviors.

In a memo from the Faculty Senate Chair at Cuyahoga Community College, Ohio:

> In response to several requests by faculty members and observations by students,
> Eastern Campus Faculty Senate has been working to make everyone more aware
> of the need for decorum and control in classrooms and throughout the campus.
> Last Fall, several faculty requested that something be done about the immature
> and sometimes obscene behavior and language from students who frequent the
> open cafeteria area. In addition, some students themselves began to complain
> about classes in which instructors did not insist on adult behavior from every-
> one throughout the class period and seemed, sometimes, not to have control of
> the class. After researching the issue, Faculty Senate learned that increasingly
> immature, and even violent, behavior is a problem nationwide at both two-year
> and four-year colleges.[12]. . . Many articles written by college faculty nationwide
> indicate (1) that college faculty members do not want to discipline their students
> as if they are the high school crowd; (2) that many college faculty, not having
> formerly experienced the need to discipline, do not know how. The reality is that
> we will have to engage in some type of discipline at times. Although most of
> the rude and disruptive behavior at Eastern Campus seems to involve students
> in 0900 classes, instructors have, in fact, experienced occasional problem be-
> haviors from students in 1000- and 2000-level classes.[13]

Disruptive, disrespectful, and disorderly students have begun to stymie
many faculty members and administrators in community colleges, colleges,
and universities. It is often expected that by the time students reach college
they will know how to behave in a classroom. However, some very promis-
ing students have even committed murder at institutions such as Harvard
(Thernstrom, 1996), Simon's Rock College of Bard, and the University of
Iowa (Matthews, 1993). Murder is the most dramatic of all the disruptive behaviors faced by college counselors and faculty. Fortunately, few counselors
or faculty members will have the experience.

Unfortunately, college instructors often experience, on a daily basis, students who are chronically late, who talk to friends during class, who eat or sleep in class, and who engage in arguments with instructors or other students (Amada, 1994). Instructors, using only the authority of their position, are no longer able to maintain decorum in their classrooms or a sense of personal safety.[14]

- From *Managing the College Classroom: Perspectives from an Introvert and an Extrovert* by Stephen W. Braden & Deborah N. Smith:

  One of the biggest challenges facing college instructors in the 21st century is classroom misbehavior. . . . One of the challenges facing instructors in the 21st century is classroom behavior leading to disciplinary action. This issue can be a day-to-day problem for some professors. Bartlett (2004) reports that incivility in today's academic culture is not the exception, but rather the norm.

- Also:

  [There is] a difficult and growing campus-wide problem . . . information that college administrators need if they are involved in: due process for disruptive students; dealing with disruptive students; disruption in residence halls; college mental health programs; student conduct codes; or staff training.[15]

- Also from "The Learning Killer: Disruptive Student Behavior in the Classroom"[16]

  A recent survey examining student learning in the college classroom found disruptive student behavior to be a major learning inhibitor. Compounding this is the realization that most college faculty are ill prepared to handle this problem. This article discusses the results of the survey as well as identifies the various types of disruptive behavior that college faculty are likely to find. Some behaviors are covert (sleeping, arriving to class late, etc.) while others are more apparent and overt (talking during class and using cellular phones). Potential solutions to the problem are also discussed. Perhaps most important, however, is the impact disruptive students can have on student retention. An unsatisfactory learning environment has been linked to students leaving a university early. . . .

  Regarding Cheating/Plagiarism: A behavior that is not only disruptive to the teacher's ability to teach, uphold standards and assess appropriate credit—is cheating and plagiarism. Surveys show that cheating in school—plagiarism, forbidden collaboration on assignments, copying homework and cheating on exams—has soared since researchers first measured the phenomenon on a broad scale at 99 colleges in the mid-1960s. The percentage of students who copied from another student during tests grew from 26 percent in 1963 to 52 percent in 1993, and the use of crib notes during exams went from 6 percent to 27 percent, according to a study conducted by Dr. Donald McCabe of Rutgers.[17] And with students' increasing ability to use technology, e.g., text messaging, the problem continues to grow in colleges.

The above are only a few examples of this spreading problem. And, these higher education discipline problems are all the more serious because they are on the increase in both frequency and severity. As the reader knows, some behaviors have become not only harmful, but tragically dangerous. Thus, the need for this book.

C. WHY IS THIS HAPPENING?

What are some of the reasons for this increasing problem in our colleges?

1. Society tends to "define deviancy down," such that what was deviant a decade ago is pushed toward the norm. What was once "unacceptable behavior" often gives way under this tendency.[18]
2. Teachers are generally doing poorly at handling high school student disruptive behavior. Fifty percent of public school teachers quit the profession within five years. When asked why they left, the most frequent reason given is the stress around classroom disruptive behavior.[19] These behaviors, not handled in the high schools, come into our college classes as high school teachers are pressured to pass these troubling students on.
3. In many colleges, entrance standards are being lowered to increase enrollment figures in order to boost registration to deal with shortfalls in the college budget. Often, a college goes for an immediate gain in enrollment by lowering admission standards in order to solve short-term cash flow problems. This is done rather than go for long-term quality standards; the latter might help the college economically in the long run, but some campuses cannot wait that long. This short-term gain in enrollment often brings with it students who are not only academically deficient, but also inadequately socialized to behave appropriately in college classrooms.
4. Students who are admitted to colleges, who under-performed in high school, have less adequate egos; they often feel somewhat inadequate compared to other more capable students. Such students walk into college classes already feeling somewhat defensive, especially if the work and course content feels a bit beyond them. When this student feels somewhat defensive, s/he often is prone to coping mechanisms that can result in withdrawal behavior. However, sometimes the coping mechanism is not

withdrawal, but instead aggressive responses (the best defense becomes an offensive reaction). For example, such a student might be prone to making wisecracks to cover his/her slipping image, especially in front of his/her peers. Thus, colleges that admit students who lack confidence about being in college tend to admit students who are prone to defensive-aggressive behavior.

5. In conjunction with the above, to save money, colleges often increase class size. Thereby, a troubled student, without much attention in a large class, easily gets "lost," and/or disruptive.

6. The college instructor is then left to handle many more students and classroom management often beyond his/her know-how.

7. Also, with economic cuts needed, often college services for students are the first supports that fall by the wayside. Students who are in need of such absent services carry their unattended problems and frustrations into the classroom.

8. As college populations become more multicultural and multilingual, diverse students can be intolerant of each other's culture, language and values, or accidentally insult the "other."

9. Students who came out of the "free" public schools may have the attitude: "Now I am paying for this college education, so now I have more freedom to do/say whatever I want."

10. K–12 teachers have *some* training in pedagogy, classroom management, and teaching methods when they are hired. However, a college teacher is often hired on the basis of only his/her knowledge of the subject matter; often, little attention is given to the professor's pedagogical skills.

11. Female college professors are often the victims of disruptive disrespect more than male college professors. Such is often the carryover of the general lack of disrespect that is still prevalent in our society's gender biases, an unjustified prejudice that students carry with them into the classroom.

Until things can be different, we must be able to contend with college students in a way that prevents college classroom disruptive behavior so that it does not impede our teaching and their learning. Regardless of how well a college instructor/professor knows his/her subject area, if s/he is not able to prevent/handle disruptive classroom behaviors and deliver effective classroom management (even if the instructor is not to blame), the instruction itself will falter.

Thus, this book has been written with concepts, implementations, interventions, and exercises specific to disruptive behavior problems in the college classroom, especially in undergraduate degree programs in higher education.

It is written from my experience and research gained from my previous book, *Preventing Classroom Discipline Problems, K–12*,[20] my articles, speeches, and my workshops on this subject. It also utilizes my experience consulting nationally in this field since 1970 and from my firsthand experience as a college classroom teacher (full professor) at an urban four-year college and university since 1970.

The kinds of disruptive behavior in college classes are sometimes similar to those found in high schools. But, more often, these college disruptive behaviors are more sophisticated, more manipulative, and often involve more clever "alibis." They are often behaviors that attempt to get through, or get by, "the cracks" in the teacher's methods, Syllabus, or personality.

So, first we must refine our understanding of the kinds of disruptive behaviors in colleges; then refine our understanding of the students who act out these hurdles to our teaching.

NOTES

1. G. H. Gallup, "Gallup Poll of Public Opinion, 1974–1983," published in *New York State United Teacher* (official publication of the New York United Federation of Teachers), vol. 43, no. 2 (November 1983), 7.

2. G. H. Gallup, "Gallup Poll," in *New York State United Teacher,* vol. 39, no. 2 (November 1979), 5.

3. D. J. Cichon and R. H. Kloff, "The Teaching Events Stress Inventory" (Paper presented at the meeting of the American Educational Research Association Conference, Toronto, Ontario (March 1978), ERIC Document Reproduction Service, no. 160, p. 662.

4. C. Kyriacou and J. Sutcliffe, "Teacher Stress: Prevalence, Sources and Symptoms," *British Journal of Educational Psychology,* 48 (1978), 159–167.

5. *New York Teacher*, May 17, 1993, 13.

6. *New York Teacher*, June 2004.

7. BBC News education reporter, April 12, 2006.

8. The *New York Times*, Feb. 1990.

9. Counseling and Student Development Center, MSC 0801, Harrisonburg, VA (January 24, 2008).

10. From http://www.oncourseworkshop.com/Miscellaneous003.htm.

11. J. Young, "Sssshhh. We're taking notes here." *The Chronicle of Higher Education* 49, 48 (2003), 29–30.

12. From http://www.oncourseworkshop.com/miscellaneous003.htm.

13. Cuyahoga Community College, "On Course" newsletter, June 2008.

14. *Journal of College Counseling*, 2001, 4(1), 49–62 © ACA. Reprinted with permission.

15. Gerald Amada, *Coping with the Disruptive College Student: A Practical Model* (Asheville, NC: College Administration Publications, 1994).

16. Alan Seidman, *Reading Improvement* 42 (2005).

17. Maura J. Casey, *New York Times* Editorial Observer, "Digging Out Roots of Cheating in High School," (October 13, 2008).

18. Senator Daniel P. Moynihan, New York State, 1990.

19. *New York Teacher*, June 2004.

20. Published by Rowman & Littlefield, 2000.

Part One

HANDLING COLLEGE
DISRUPTIVE BEHAVIORS

Chapter One

Disruptive Behaviors in College Classrooms

A. Who Are These Disruptive Students? Student Categories
B. Disruptive Behaviors Typical of Each Student Category
C. Disruptive Behaviors Regardless of Student Category
D. Extreme Harmful/Disruptive Behaviors — Isolated and Campus-wide

As we briefly discussed above, due to a lowering of standards, economic pressures in higher education, and a sometimes disrespectful student body passed along into colleges, college instructors are more often encountering student disruptive behaviors in their classes. We need to take a look at all these behaviors and consider the best way to both prevent their occurrence and how to handle them.

Here is how we will proceed:

A. First, it will be helpful to characterize the students who tend to be disruptive into categories. These descriptions of types of students will give us a better understanding of the causes of these behaviors, besides the specific behaviors themselves. Of course, any brief description of a group is an oversimplification; but such will provide us with a perspective to guide our constructive reactions to disruptive behaviors. And, it should be said explicitly in case I may be misunderstood below, that ethnicity, race, or economic class has no correlation with membership in these student categories.
B. We will then discuss specific disruptive behaviors typical of each of these student categories.
C. Then, we will identify college disruptive behaviors that may arise *regardless* of the student category.
D. Finally, we will discuss some extreme disruptive behaviors.

A. WHO ARE THESE DISRUPTIVE STUDENTS?

I've taught college students in the City University of New York, New York City since 1970. Over these years, the population went from mainly middle class white students to poor working class, multicultural, multiracial students. I've also watched the college's admission criteria go from high standards to completely "open admissions," supplemented by a large enrollment in departments working on remediation and study skills. Then, after years of "open admissions," I watched the college go to a rescinding of this policy, more stringent admission standards, elimination of many remediation courses, and an attempt, again, to maintain high standards. But, as reality would have it, the latter more stringent stance is always pressured to be lowered again by concerns about high student attrition, inadequate funding, and an effort (sometimes any effort) to increase enrollment. These "rises and falls" are typical of many institutions of higher learning, especially public institutions, in the United States, and internationally as well.

During these "rises and falls," you can legitimately describe certain categories in these student populations that (though oversimplified) can help us better understand student disruptive behavior in college classes.

Student Categories

1. "The Mountain Climbers"

These are the students that I not only have a very high respect for, but find often inspirational. They are frequently first- or second-generation immigrants. Often, they are working parents (sometimes without spouses). They often come from a difficult economic situation, and are trying to be the first in their families to ever go to college, let alone graduate with a college degree. In almost gladiator circumstances, living in sometimes drug-ridden neighborhoods, they dedicate themselves to their children and to the tasks of a college education in order to earn a college diploma and a successful career. Many of these students, e.g., education majors, endeavor to graduate and eventually go back to their neighborhoods "to save kids like they were." Teaching these enduring "mountain-climbers" gives back such meaning and intimacy to the job of teaching them that it is nothing but a privilege to work with them. They often give back in just pure inspiration more than what we give them in our mere lectures.

2. "The Well-to-Do"

I don't just mean students who are well-off economically or come from middle or upper class families. I mean students whose parents went to college, are well read, and, for example, had the time and circumstances to read to their children when they were preschoolers, did homework with them, and consistently encouraged and developed their learning skills and values regarding getting a good education. These students are often socially-emotionally confident and display agile cognitive skills.

3. "The Game Players"

These students know the "student-teacher game." They know how to be a "student" and how to get the teacher's attention and approval. They know how to play this role to the particular personality of the teacher, who they perceptively try to "win over." These students want to "win" their best grade in the course, and are often artful manipulators. They are often not motivated by any intrinsic desire for an education. They are often, instead, motivated by wanting to "just get by" or to make a lot of money some day, or have great status. They can argue well and long, know how to "brownnose," or "get over on a teacher," and even how to emotionally bribe or threaten a teacher—sometimes bordering on racial, ethical, or harassment issues in general. It is not that these students are mean spirited, or hostile, or that they don't care about getting a degree. It is just that they have often had such a hard time at living and surviving that they have developed "survival skills," and "street smarts." They have come to find that being manipulative, even lying, is often more "successful" than honest hard work.

Unfortunately, these students, as a by-product of their manipulative style, often front a "cool" image. However, in fact, as a result of this manipulative style, they often have low egos and have few friends who really trust them. As a result, often they are emotionally "alone," very often fail at school, at home, or in having a full life (even if they figure out ways to accumulate material goods). Such students are often susceptible to being drug addicted, alcoholic, or substance abusers in general. Probably, no one college student completely fits this description above. Instead, what is usually the case is that a student has a tendency to be "the game player" sometimes. But, also, sometimes does honest work. When he/she becomes the former, then, we will need to handle his/her brand of "disruptive" behavior.

4. "The Immature"

These students are not necessarily manipulators. When they say that they don't understand or forgot . . . , they are sincere. They usually are intellectually and/or emotionally underdeveloped. They have trouble with learning, organizational and reasoning skills, have poor work and study habits, are shy, and have low self-esteem. They may have come from families who never modeled or nurtured these skills, nor their emotional development. These students often want to learn, and do honest work, but, sadly, really have difficulties with college work and its social environment.

5. *"The Learning Disabled"*

This descriptive category is never simple nor clearly definable. They are students who may, for example, be dyslexic, have motor perception problems, or even have emotional disturbances that affect and/or cause educational problems. These students may even be "mature"—they are not in category 4 above—but often have psychological or physiological, chemical imbalances that are obstacles to their learning.

Of course, all of the above student categories are only oversimplified generalizations. They are not actual, real groups of students. In a way, they are *styles of behaving.* Any one student may, at various times, fit any number of these styles of behaving. However, these student categories can help us characterize specific disruptive behaviors that we may need to deal with in college classes.

B. DISRUPTIVE BEHAVIORS TYPICAL OF EACH STUDENT CATEGORY

Again, we will talk in oversimplified terms, now regarding behaviors typical of each student category. These broad strokes are meant as guidelines for the appropriate college teacher reactions in order to prevent and handle college-level disruptive behaviors.

(A word of caution: We will need to decide which of these behaviors is not just disruptive to you personally—a "miscall"—but truly disruptive to your teaching and the learning of the rest of the class—"real discipline problems." Notice, it will be important to realize in advance that to handle all disruptions appropriately, we will have to make this important distinction. But, more on this distinction later in chapter 2.)

For now, I will describe some of the potentially disruptive behaviors that are typical of each category of student described above. *The page numbers provided indicate where the reader may find suggestions for handling these specific behaviors.*

1. "The Mountain Climbers"

a. Since some of these students may be bilingual, you may find them asking you to go slower, or repeat something again because they are having language difficulties. (**39**)

b. Or, at times, they may whisper to a friend during a lecture or even pass notes to consult regarding translating your instructions or lecture. (**39**)

c. They may often need further instructions about a missed lecture or homework assignment because they couldn't attend class (or came late, or had to leave class early) due to their need to take care of a problem at their job, or with their family or children. (**39**)

d. They may sometimes need to bring their young child to class with them because they cannot afford to get child care when the college is in session, especially when the public schools are not. (**40**)

2. "The Well-to-Do"

e. They may rest securely on their emotional confidence, and not be shy to challenge you regarding your rules, grading policy, and your presentation of the subject matter—often all with great cognitive agility. (**40**)

3. "The Game Players"

f. These students may often greet you with subtle compliments, or even do you favors, sometimes small, even unwanted. (**40–41**)

g. They may "yes" you a lot, "thank you" a lot, to the point that you don't really know what the student is really thinking. (**41**)

h. They may try to figure out the answer you want to hear, rather than really go through any reasoning process. They may do this no matter how much you try to teach reasoning skills, or ask you rhetorical questions wearing a "poker face." (**41**)

i. They may argue about their lateness, absence, or your grading with great excuses and sob stories to bolster whatever wrangling they can come up with to bend you. (**45–46**)

j. If they think you can be made to feel guilty, they will imply (or even state explicitly) that you are being racist, sexist, or just unfair. Some will even threaten you to go to the "the higher-ups" about the matter. (**46–47**)

k. They will either show you resentment or grave sadness (sulk) in order to move you. (**41**)

l. If the above is unsuccessful, and they are confident enough, they may call out, cheat . . . , and generally bother other students' learning. (**47–53**)

4. "The Immature"

m. They may raise their hands often and ask you to repeat something, or ask what seems like, from your point of view, to be an "unnecessary" question. (**41**)

n. They may often forget your instructions, or what you explained. (**41**)
o. Their reasoning may be swayed by emotion and/or be full of fallacies. (**41**)
p. They may not be able to explain, or answer "*why* questions," but only fall into giving examples—where they often believe that just one case proves their point. (**41–42**)
q. They may be so shy that you cannot get them to respond in class. And, when they respond on paper, their writing approaches illiteracy. (**42**)

5. "The Learning Disabled"

r. These students may need you to repeat something because they have a hearing or cognitive processing impairment. (**42**)
s. Or they may be late because of a physical disability. (**42**)
t. Or they may need more time to fulfill an assignment or take a test because of a writing or reading disability (though deceptively, they may have quite competent oral skills). (**42**)

Besides all of these above behaviors per student category, we also have these, regardless of the student category:

C. DISRUPTIVE BEHAVIORS REGARDLESS OF STUDENT CATEGORY

A. Not respecting the rights of other students' viewpoints. (**49**)
B. Monopolizing the discussion. (**49**)
C. Talking when you or another student is speaking. (**50**)
D. Constant questions that interfere with your teaching. (**50**)
E. Withdrawn, inattentive, or sleeping in class, or reading or doing another subject in your class. (**43**)
F. Eating in class. (**50–51**)
G. Making noise with papers, or by tapping a pen or pencil. (**51**)
H. Coming to class late or leaving early. (**52**)
I. Using pagers, cell phones, and iPods in the classroom. (**52**)
J. Inappropriate demands or too many demands for your time and attention. (**43**)
K. Poor personal hygiene (e.g., offensive body odor). (**44**)
L. Students text messaging each other during your teaching. (**44**)

D. EXTREME HARMFUL/DISRUPTIVE BEHAVIORS—
ISOLATED AND CAMPUS-WIDE

M. Use of profanity or pejorative language in class. (**52–53**)

N. Intoxication, or high on drugs, or selling drugs. (**53–54**)

O. Verbal abuse (e.g., taunting, badgering, intimidation). (**54**)

P. Harassment (e.g., use of "fighting words"). (**54**)

Q. Cheating on tests. (**54–56**)

R. Plagiarism. (**57**)

Campus-wide

S. Threats to harm oneself or others. (**57–58**)

T. Physical violence, assault, carrying weapons. (**58–61**)

U. Sexual assaults/rape. (**61–67**)

V. Binge Drinking. (**67–68**)

I think that the above lists of disruptive behaviors are near exhaustive for college classes. (If you have come across a behavior that I have not mentioned above here, feel free to email me at Hokaja@aol.com.)

Now, we need to work on the best strategies to both prevent/curtail and handle these behaviors.

Chapter Two

Distinguishing "Miscalls" from Discipline Problems

A. An Important Distinction: Miscall vs. Discipline Problem
B. An Online Video Demonstration: *Noticing Miscalls*
C. Fifteen Typical Miscalls
D. Handling Typical Miscalls
E. Handling Miscalls by Student Category
F. Handling Students Who:
   Ask you to repeat; come late; leave early; whisper; bring children to class; challenge; manipulate; blurt out; can't write; are disabled
G. Handling Miscalls Regardless of Student Category:
   Students who are withdrawn; sleep; do other homework in class; demand; text message

Before we can discuss how to prevent and handle all the disruptive behaviors that we delineated in the last chapter, we must first make an important distinction, a hard one to digest and one that is counterintuitive.

A. AN IMPORTANT DISTINCTION: MISCALL VS. DISCIPLINE PROBLEM

Not all behaviors that *you* find disruptive should be handled with an assertive response from you, especially in front of the class. Or, not all behaviors that are disruptive to you are "discipline problems." Some disruptive behaviors, if handled that way, are what I will call *miscalls*. They should *not* be "gone after on the spot"; instead, they should be handled a different way. And these "miscalls" when acted out by the teacher are often more disruptive to the teaching/learning of the class than the behavior that the teacher reprimanded in the first place.

To help us nail down this new way of seeing things, one has to re-form our understanding of when a behavior is a real disruptive behavior: "discipline problem." Again, this is not easy to do—since we all tend to teach the way we were taught. And, we have been taught this *miscalling way to react* for years and years, ever since we were in kindergarten, or before, in our families.

We need to re-form our reactions. Look again at what I am saying:

Not all behaviors that *you* find disruptive should be handled with an assertive response from you, especially in front of the class. Or, not all behaviors that are disruptive to you are "discipline problems." Some disruptive behaviors, if handled that way, are what I will call *miscalls*. They should not be "reprimanded on the spot"; instead, they should be handled a different way.

But, when is it a real "discipline problem"? OK, stated conversely, it is NOT a "miscall," it IS a real discipline problem when: *it is a behavior (not merely the expression of a feeling) that disrupts (or is potentially disruptive to) the learning of the rest of the class (not just the learning of the disrupter), or disrupts the role responsibilities of the teacher (not just the personal feelings of the teacher).*

But it is a "miscall" when: *the teacher assertively, with authoritative irritation, reprimands a student during the class when:*

A. *the student's behavior is not disrupting (or potentially disrupting) the learning of the rest of the class*
B. *(though the learning of that individual student may be disrupted),*
C. *and/or this behavior is not disrupting the role responsibilities of the teacher (though it may be personally disruptive to the teacher).*
   - *In other words, this kind of behavior (A., B., C.) can be handled differently: e.g., can be side-stepped, handled later, not made to be a big deal, not focused on, even overlooked. . . .*
   - *And the teacher can keep on teaching.*

To mention just one example of a clear miscall: To go after a student who is not paying attention, e.g., looking out the window is a miscall: "John, are you in this class or not?!" To reprimand this student during the class—especially with irritation, or worse, sarcasm, especially when no one else in the class was noticing him, when you could have just gone on with your teaching (with your hurt ego)—is a miscall.

Sure, his learning is going out the window, but when he has taken your test, if you have good tests and guard against cheating, and your lectures are relevant to the tests that you give . . . he will have been handled by the latter.

Since he is only disrupting his own learning, neither the learning of the rest of the class nor your teaching, really, to go after him would make YOU the most disruptive in the class. (You say, "What if they all start looking out the window?" Then, it is your teaching and teaching methods, Syllabi, tests, etc., that need remediation, not the students. We will help with all of these in later chapters.)

Notice again: for most of us the example above is counterintuitive. Many of us reflexively respond to whatever is "disruptive" to us without really making or noticing this distinction between a miscall and a real "discipline problem." We must face the fact that if we are to better handle "disruptive behaviors," we must not only re-train our perceptions but also our responses. And then practice making this distinction and then practice responding differently.

The following fictional little story is helpful in realizing the deleterious effects of making miscalls: *Mr. Blurt is in the middle of frying some eggs on the stove, when suddenly the entire shelf above the stove begins to dislodge from the wall and fall. Mr. Blurt immediately gets very annoyed and anxious about how disruptive this is to his meal, and impulsively grabs for a hammer in a nearby drawer. Without thinking, he strikes angrily with the hammer at the fastener that has become loose in the wall. He now notices things are now worse. The plaster wall has begun to break up and the shelf is even weaker. He notices that the supposed nail that he struck with the hammer was actually a screw. In his haste, he has struck a screw with a hammer, instead of using a screwdriver. But, after all, a screwdriver would have taken too long. Mr. Blurt, in his haste, could not be bothered with fitting the end of a screwdriver carefully to the notch of a screw, and turning it slowly. But, now the situation is much worse. The blow of the hammer has closed up the notch in file screw and cracked the wall it was screwed into. As the shelf begins to fall into Mr. Blurt's food, his meal is even more disrupted!*

Miscalling a situation a "discipline problem" when it might be better handled in another way is like *hitting a screw with a hammer*. When classroom situations annoy us, we get anxious and disrupted. We want to stop the behavior as fast as possible. So, like Mr. Blurt, we blurt out whatever impulsively comes to our minds: "John, you back there with your head on your desk, pay attention! What do you think this is . . . ?"

At this point, the entire class has stopped taking notes and is now looking, maybe even laughing, at John. John then probably engages you in a two minute argument that begins with: "Hey, I wasn't bothering anybody. What are you getting on me for? Get off my case!" And on, and on. . . . Things have gotten worse. Now, your teaching has really gotten disrupted, and probably—the most disruptive behavior in the classroom was yours!

B. AN ONLINE VIDEO DEMONSTRATION:
NOTICING MISCALLS

The best way to *nail down* (or should I say *screw down*) this distinction is to watch the mistake being made on this video. (In the video, that is me; only I am a bit older now.) The "students" in the scenes are actually real teachers who are role-playing disruptive students, *their* disruptive students. Most of them were having problems with students who were in high school, so they role-played *them*. However, the video is still useful for understanding this mistake: *miscalls*. You can imagine your own mistakes for college students.

The video is about six minutes long. Go to www.classroommanagement online.com/miscalls. To view the video, you will be asked for a username; type in: PROFSEEMAN (all caps). You will also be asked for the password, which is 6666. You may have to enter these twice. Now you can view the video "Demo on Miscalls."

I hope that the video made the concept of "miscalls" even clearer for you. Notice that the definition of a miscall has several parts:

A. The student's behavior is not disrupting (or potentially disrupting) the learning of the rest of the class
B. (though the learning of that individual student may be disrupted).
C. And/or this behavior is not disrupting the role responsibilities of the teacher
D. (though it may be personally disruptive to the teacher).

    a. In other words, this kind of behavior (A, B, C) can be side-stepped, handled later, or no big deal, not focused on, even overlooked;
    b. and the teacher can keep on teaching.

However, we can notice that our definitions of "discipline problem" and "miscall" do not tell us, by themselves, what a particular situation is and how it is best handled. We still need to carefully judge whether each situation comes under a "miscall" or a "discipline problem." But we now have guidelines to make this judgment. We can ask, for instance:

- "Is this behavior disruptive to our role responsibilities as teacher, or only to ourselves as a person?"
- "Need it disrupt our ability to teach, determine fair grades, protect other students from injury, protect personal or school property . . . ?" No? Then, it's probably a personal disruption, a miscall if treated with disciplinary action.

- "Is it a behavior or merely the expression of a feeling?" Sometimes it may be difficult to decide, but these kinds of questions can be guidelines for the decision.
- "Is the student only disrupting his own education, or the education of others?" If it is the latter, it is a discipline problem. If it is only the former, then it is probably handled best as an education problem.

Generally, such education problems are best handled by either finding better ways to motivate the student or by showing the student how his or her behavior may result in poorer grades, e.g., by seeing the student after class or at an office hour. If your tests are about what you teach in class, then grade evaluations are a way to handle the student who is not disrupting anyone else's education but his own. In this way, the student bears the responsibility of his actions without disrupting your teaching or the rest of the class, or YOU disrupting the class by wrongly going after him during class.

Let's also notice that we need not consider the intention of the student in making these determinations. Students often are prone to try to manipulate their way out of trouble. For example: John says, "But I was only talking to Sue to get the homework."

If teachers' decisions always involved them as judge and jury, especially about non-empirical matters, they would never be able to make clear decisions. The decision as to whether it is a discipline problem or not is determined by judging observable behavior. Is the student who talks to Sue disrupting the learning of the class and your teaching? And, it does not last just for a second? Is it going on and on? Yes? Then, your response to this student may take something like this form: "John, please see me after class." Then, you may say something like: " John, I don't care why you were talking to Sue. When you keep talking to someone in the middle of my teaching, you disrupt the learning of those students around you, and my train of thought, and thus my teaching this class. Either don't be absent so you won't need to get the homework from Sue, or call her, or ask her before class, or after class, but not while I'm teaching. Do you understand?"

The above approach to this disruptive behavior of "talking while you are teaching" is a better "screwdriver" than a "hammer" in the middle of the class.

You are not alone with making these miscalls. I have delineated at least fifteen typical miscalls, where a "screwdriver" would have been better than a "hammer." We will discuss more of these better "screwdriver methods" in section D below. But for now, here are:

C. FIFTEEN TYPICAL MISCALLS

1. The Withdrawn Student

If a student is withdrawn while you are teaching, but not disrupting either the learning of the rest of the class or you as teacher, to reprimand this student in front of the class would be a miscall. The student might have his head down on his desk in the back of the room, or be reading a book not related to your course, or looking out the window. If he draws attention to himself, and the other students become distracted, then he is a discipline problem. If, however, he's not disrupting the learning of anyone else but his own, then he is either an education problem or a guidance problem, but not a discipline problem.

2. The Overreacted-to Rule

A rule is obviously a restriction that has been generalized to cover many situations. However, many rules originate from one instance that is obviously appropriate, and then are spread over too many instances inappropriately. That's why we often need to interject into a rule sometimes exceptions: "But, of course, if x is the case, then it's OK if you don't. . . ." These exceptions to our rules are made in order to correct our overreaction to, or exaggeration of, a rule.

One example of a commonly overreacted-to rule is the "no food" rule. Probably the rule originates appropriately with a student who begins to eat something like potato chips in class. Obviously eating such food in class is noisy and, thereby, disruptive to the learning of the rest of the class, and you as teacher. Such food is also prone to be passed around the room. Objecting to this situation of eating potato chips in class is thus not a miscall. But, what about sucking on a sourball? Or, a cough drop? What if a student says, "It's medicine." Do we then revert to the rule, "No food except if you have a note from a doctor"? What about the student who is sucking loudly on a rubber band? When you get annoyed at her, she then responds, "But I'm not eating any food!" Or, chewing gum?

In order to enforce the "no food" rule do we inspect every student's mouth?! Obviously, if we proceed this way we are on the trail of an overreacted-to rule. The "no food" rule was designed so that eating food in class does not disrupt the learning of the class. What we really want is that students do not eat or suck or chew on anything that disturbs the class. Then, whether they are sucking on medicine or not (even if they have three doctors' notes), making noise that disrupts the class means they can be a "discipline problem."

Perhaps, what we want to enforce is something like: "The main thing is that I will not tolerate any eating in class that disturbs our learning. You can eat a whole turkey if you choose, just don't let me or anyone hear you or see you and want some."

That's the rule. This rule is more enforceable, and is one that is less prone to miscalls. (Of course, you need to enforce a rule here that *you* believe in [see chapter 4, section D] after you think it all out. For example, you may want allow them to drink *water* in your class. Or, you may not permit food that spills. In any case, decide the clear rule. Then, try to not overreact, nor have a rule that has you spending class time being judge and jury.

Furthermore, if you worry that gum will be stuck to desks, that is a separate issue. Do you want to support the janitorial work at your college and the janitors? Yes? Fine. But gum chewing, in and of itself, is not a "discipline problem." It irks you? Do you want to take on this job, besides all your teaching responsibilities? OK, good luck.)

3. The "I've Got to Win Their Feelings" Need

Obviously, a student who grimaces at you because she is bored may be a sign that she needs to be motivated or that she is annoyed by you or even your teaching. However, since she is not disrupting the learning of the rest of the class, she's not a discipline problem. You probably feel insulted that she's bored with your teaching, but that's a feeling of being disrupted as "person," not as teacher.

You can't always win students' feelings. As normal human beings we like to have students smile when we are doing our wonderful teaching, or answer our questions with the proper affect in their tone of voice, or show excitement when we perform, and laugh at our jokes. As teachers, if we feel this need *to win their feelings*, we are prone to slowly get annoyed at mere expressions of feelings that are not disruptive to the learning of the rest of the class or ourselves as teacher. It is then that we are prone to make this kind of miscall.

4. The "I Need Their Attention" Syndrome

You are writing notes on the front blackboard as you explain something. The students are generally listening to you and copying the notes from the blackboard. At one point, you run out of room on the front blackboard and walk over to continue your notes on the side blackboard. All the students' heads turn as they follow you and your notes to the side blackboard—except for Tom. Does this slightly annoy you? Keep in mind that it is not true that, as teacher, you always need their attention. Maybe Tom needed to pay attention more to the front blackboard (he hadn't finished copying those notes) rather than to look at you and the side blackboard?

As people, we like to be looked at when we talk. Sometimes, however, students need to look at their notes, their pen, or think and look off to the side. Sometimes looking at their notes is more educational than looking at you. Sometimes you may really need their attention to point out to them a specific line on your blackboard diagram, or to illustrate a nonverbal point in your teaching. But it's not true that you, as teacher, always need their attention. Try to keep this in mind; otherwise, you may build up annoyances here and be prone to reaching for a "hammer," wrongly.

5. The "My Ego Is Hurt" Reaction

This miscall is just another form of 3 and 4 above. Sometimes we tend to reprimand a student not because s/he is disrupting the learning of the class or our teaching, but because s/he has hurt our ego. An example of this is the student who is quietly doing her Math homework in your History course. Similarly, we may inadvertently be prone to be irritated at a student who has not been laughing at our jokes. Or we spend hours before class preparing our "great detective lesson." However, at the very first clue we give, Tom figures it all out and gives the answer (even properly raises his hand). Our entire great creative teaching is blown away, our ego is shot down, and we're prone to be angry.

Here, we can we allow our "person" to set off our reaching for a teacher "hammer." Then, we may be the most disruptive person in our class and also, perhaps, damage any good relationship we need to have with our students.

6. "They're Interfering with My Getting My Teaching Plan Done" Reaction

You're a professor of history and you're up to the causes of World War II, while another professor, teaching another section of the same course, is up to the aftermath of World War II.

You're reading/explaining your notes to the class about the causes of World War II as fast as you can, and the students are taking notes as fast as they can. Suddenly, Tom raises his hand. You call on him and he says, "All this stuff reminds me of how fights can start at home, like because of jealousy and control, right?" You respond, "Tom, we're not talking about home and families. We're discussing a war with Germany and its allies. Now, please get back to your notes." You have probably made a miscall.

Sometimes students will try to pull us off difficult learning problems because they feel uninterested or frustrated. However, sometimes they interject a question or comment because what you are teaching reminds them of their lives. Obviously, the latter reaction is educational. After all, we spend so much of our time and energy trying to make our subject matter relevant. We should feel glad if this relevance just happens. Research has shown that learning that is not related to any significant affect in the learner's life is seldom remembered.[1]

As teachers, we must be able to treat the associations students make to the content of our teaching as useful connections for learning. Of course, we cannot go from World War II to discussing families for the next hour. However, we can channel this relevant association, ask students to incorporate it into their notes, and use it to drive home a point in the curriculum. And, we can always ask, if you are not sure whether to follow this *digression*: "John, how does this comment you just made relate to what I was teaching? It rang a bell for you? Please explain."

What we must try to remember when we have this reaction: "They're interfering with my getting my teaching plan done" that it is not always our teaching that matters, it is their learning. If we have only ten minutes left to the class, and we quickly dictate all the causes of World War II, and they get them down into their notes, we are fooling ourselves if we believe that now they've "got" the causes of World War II.

Notes are not learnings. If your train gets from New York to Chicago faster than the other teacher, but no one is on the train, you are not a good teacher. Sometimes you may have to go from New York to Philadelphia and then to Chicago in order to pick up your passengers. Sometimes you may have to discuss Tommy's seeming digression about families in order to have students really understand wars. Tommy's digression isn't a digression, especially if many students' minds in your class were also wandering in that direction. After all, one main reason we teach History is to learn from the past to relate these events to the understanding of the present and possible future.

Of course, we must use our judgment here. Some students' questions are really digressions, remarks that *are* off the subject. We must learn to ask ourselves, "Is this remark helpful to their learning? Or am I annoyed only because it's off my lecture notes, and I'm behind?" If the remark is helpful to learning, try to channel it. For example: you can take notes on Tom's remark on families; there's nothing wrong with teachers taking notes on the class discussion too—to be used by you in your next lecture. Your taking notes will also help you keep track of what you taught in the last class, and perhaps prevent you from making this kind of miscall.

7. Displaced Anger

Obviously, to get angry at a student who does not deserve your anger is to treat someone with disciplinary action inappropriately. This miscall occurs when we misplace our anger. It is usually easier and safer for us to get annoyed with students than it is to express our anger toward, e.g., our boss or spouse. Therefore, students are apt to be the target of anger that has been displaced. You leave home annoyed at your spouse and take it out on this student in your History class. Or you're angry with the Chair of your department, so you walk into your class "ready to get someone."

It is at these times that "screws" may appear as "nails" needing the blow of a hammer. We need to be able to identify the source of our annoyance and not displace these irritations. Sometimes sharing your feelings with a friend may help. Or, sometimes, you might even mention this to the class: "Class, I have a headache today, and am annoyed about something that happened about an hour ago, but nothing to do with you. So if I sound irritable, I don't mean it at you." This kind of openness may help you get rid of, or at least put aside, your irritation. And, by guarding against making this kind of miscall, you may even promote a better relationship between you and the class.

8. "I'm Tired of Trying to Be Understanding All the Time" Reaction

We all know this feeling. You're teaching American History. A student asks a question that shows that she still doesn't understand what you mean by "imports." You patiently re-explain it. You explain it again, this time even clearer. Then, someone asks: "Isn't that, like, short for things that are *important?*" That's it! You answer him sarcastically: "Sure, your comment is un-important!" Then, she makes a wisecrack at your sarcasm: "So are you!" The whole class laughs. Now it's war!

This miscall occurs most when we're tired, or feel behind in our work, or when we're at the end of the day or semester and beginning to run out of patience. Teaching is exhausting. It's not just the teaching that is so difficult, it's the listening, understanding, empathizing, being careful, being patient, etc. However, if we can feel this miscall coming, we can prevent ourselves from creating even more disruptions.

9. The Mirror Effect

All of us are prone to overreact to certain students. We get more annoyed at certain students than is appropriate. Sometimes this kind of reaction has nothing to do with displaced anger or our ego. Instead, certain students just bug us, like the one who always tries to give the correct answer but in a cute way. She doesn't really disrupt the class or your teaching; it's just her "trying to be cute all the time" gets to you.

Well, does she remind you of you, or how you used to be, or someone you know in your personal life or your family—who irritates you? Sometimes, what we don't like about ourselves bugs us when we see it in other people, or these students remind us of our fights with our, e.g., brother.

If so, you are prone to get annoyed at this student, and commit this kind of miscall: "the mirror effect." This can happen during our teaching and, thus, be the source of an inappropriate "hammer blow."

10. The "I Need to Control" Reaction

We all need some control over our lives, our jobs, and our own reactions. Often we can't seem to get control over our reactions. So, sometimes, instead, we revert to trying to control those things or people that make us so reactive. Certain little things just drive us crazy. Our reactions may be irrational, but we feel justified in trying to have things our own way anyway. Some teachers get upset when they see students constantly fiddling with their hair, or slumping in their seats. Or some teachers feel like stopping their teaching if the seats in the class are not aligned straightly.

We all have our little hang-ups. These are areas in which we need more control than is educationally necessary in order to do our jobs well. These reactions are personal sensitivities that need not be "disruptive" to your teaching. We need to be aware of these irrational feelings and not coerce our students to accommodate to our unusual sensitivities, nor should we build up irritations that might affect our teaching delivery. We need to keep a watch on this reaction, or we will come off in an irritating way to our students. Or worse, we may commit a miscall. Careful, do not use your power to make yourself comfortable beyond your teaching responsibilities. To do so is to make a miscall that can turn your students into enemies. If you cannot work out your sensitivities, at least talk to the student who is bugging you person-to-person, "Tom, could you move your seat in a little? You're not doing anything wrong; it just bugs me when things are out of line. OK? Thank you."

11. The "Steam" for "Smoke" Mistake

If you've ever been driving on a city street and suddenly noticed what seems to be a fire on the road in front of you, you'll understand this miscall well. Usually, what looked like smoke pouring from beneath the street turns out to be only steam from an open steam pipe under the city streets. Sometimes we make an analogous mistake in our classrooms. We use a PowerPoint presentation, or role-play something in order to rouse the interest of our students.

If we are successful, students begin to participate: asking many questions, offering their comments, and hopefully getting excited.

However, motivated students are less quiet than bored students. If you treat this excitement as if it is disruptive noise, you will have mistaken "steam" for "smoke." Steam is a form of energy. Smoke is usually a sign of fire. It's best to *channel* steam so it can do work. We may need to make sure that when students are highly motivated that they not call out too much so that everyone can follow the discussion that you energized. We may even request that, "All of you who wish to speak must first write down your answer." Or, maybe even: "Folks, if you want to make a comment on this topic, you have to first briefly summarize what the last student said before you give your opinion."

It would be a miscall, however, to excite your class and then get annoyed with students who show their excitement. A student who begins to monopolize the discussion, or does not respect others' comments, or who shouts obsceni-ties . . . might be exhibiting "smoke." This behavior may need to be extin-guished before it becomes "fire," before his behavior disrupts the learning of others. However, we must be careful to distinguish "smoke" from "steam."

12. The Venting for Cursing Mistake

The best way to explain this kind of miscall is by telling a true story told to me by a teacher years ago. It seems that this nine-year-old boy was in an art class in a parochial school. He was apparently painting a picture of his own yellow house with a blue sky in the background. The nun who was teaching the class began coming around to see each child's painting. The student (let's call him Tommy) began to get nervous and turned around to see if the nun was coming. As he turned around, he accidentally knocked over a jar of red paint all over his painting. When Tommy saw the paint spill, he blurted out, "Oh, shit!" The nun heard him. Tommy covered his mouth, but it was too late. The words had already come out. The nun grabbed Tommy by his collar and pulled him out of the class shouting, "How dare you talk that way in my classroom? I'll have you suspended for this!"

She took Tommy to the principal's office and demanded that the principal call Tommy's mother immediately and inform her that Tommy would be kept after school for a suspension hearing. Apparently the principal yielded to the nun's demand and called the mother right there. When the mother answered the phone, the principal said, "Sorry to bother you, Mrs. Smith, but I'm call-ing to tell you that we'll have to keep Tommy after school today because of what he did." The mother immediately responded, "Oh shit, what did he do?"

What Tommy actually did was only to vent his frustration and upset. The nun assumed that "Oh shit" was equivalent to cursing. She apparently took any expression of a "dirty" word as a personal curse at her. However, clearly, "Shit on you!" is not "Oh shit!" Cursing is different from venting. The former is at someone in order to hurt him, while the latter is usually an impulsive expression of some kind of anger. We must be careful not to mistake venting for cursing. Some students, e.g., raised on the streets of large cities, are not even aware of the transgression that we want to reprimand, "What the f—— did I say?"

In your college classroom Tom opens his backpack and suddenly everything spills onto the floor. He says, "Shit!" Here, if a student accidentally says a word society deems "dirty" (after all, there are really no inherently dirty words), it might be best in some cases to: a) just let the expression slide; b) say: "Please . . ." and show some disfavor; c) perhaps remark that some words are not appropriate for this environment. But, it would be a miscalled "hammer" reaction if you stop the class and reprimand this venting behavior in front of the class. Keep in mind: the class probably isn't upset about this "dirty" word; they probably have heard that stuff, and worse, hundreds of times.

However, if we can realize that Tom's venting is just venting, it's obvious that the most disruptive behavior might be your reprimand at him in front of the class. So if we're smart we can respond, "Now class, just settle down." "Tom, sorry about your backpack." And thereby you pass by an entire mountain out of a molehill.

Now you ask: What if it is not venting but real cursing? Well, the one that you may be thinking of is: "F—— you!" at you. Right? Yes, this would NOT be a miscall; it would be a real disruptive behavior. However, let's ask: How would such a situation materialize? The answer is probably that a student got so angry at you midst your teaching that s/he now curses at you: "F—— you!" But, what would cause such a reaction? The answer is you probably said/did something to him/her that either felt insulting or demanded something that made him/her feel very uncomfortable *in front of the whole class.*

Well, don't do that. Do not say/do things to a student in front of the class that is insulting or makes him feel uncomfortable in front of his peers. "F—— you!" is the "push back at you" for your "insulting push at him" in front of the class. Do not do that. If you have any irritation, demand, "push" you need to express to a student, always wait and ask: "Please see me after class."

13. The Prejudicial Mistake

It is obvious that it is an extremely unprofessional miscall to reprimand a student simply because of his/her race, creed, religion, gender, or sexual orientation. However, we need to be reminded that prejudice often originates in anxiety turned to anger and then generalized (Gordon Allport, *The Nature of Prejudice*, 1954). We are all raised with various kinds of prejudices that sometimes flare up in our unaware, biased judgments. The only safeguard against prejudice (until our society itself is cured) is awareness. We have the responsibility as helping professionals to continually ask ourselves, "Am I overreacting or judging unfairly because of a prejudice I may have?" Along these same lines, we must take care that we are not playing favorites with those we are attracted to.

14. Holding a Grudge

Similarly, we should not judge a student simply based on his past history, or on our leftover anger that we have with him/her from how s/he was, e.g., yesterday. If s/he did something that warranted a reprimand or, e.g. a lower grade on a previous test and it was handled, then: it is over. To be fair, we need to start with a new, clean slate. We must be careful that our decision about whether or not to reprimand him/her now is based on his/her current behavior.

15. The Punishing the Education Problem Mistake

Should you reprimand Tom in front of the class if he obviously has not done the reading you assigned? We've already decided that if he's bored, or withdrawn, or even sleeping, he is probably an education problem who is disrupting only his own learning; he is not a discipline problem. But, if he hasn't done what you asked the class to do, isn't he then a discipline problem? Is his having not done his homework disruptive to anyone else but himself? Is he disrupting the learning of the class? Is this neglect of his work disruptive to your ability to teach? It seems that this behavior is only disruptive to the rest of the class if you call attention to it and spend class time on Tom's neglect.

If your reading assignments are not just "busy work," but actually help students learn, and if your tests validly measure the learning you have taught and assigned for homework, then students who do not do their homework should do poorly on your tests. These poor grades can be the deterrent—rather than your counterproductive reprimand in front of the class. "But," you reply, "what if they don't care about their grades?" Then, our reprimands or punishments, especially in front of the class, will in no way cultivate their care. However, such reprimands or punishments of an education problem may produce coerced behavior, resentment, and further withdrawal. "But," you reply, "what if they can score high on my tests without doing the homework? What then?" Then, obviously, the students find that your homework is irrelevant to your tests. Then, it is you the teacher who needs to go to work, not the students who need to be reprimanded for not doing the assignments.

D. HANDLING TYPICAL MISCALLS

Now that we know that these above behaviors are prone to be handled incorrectly—as miscalls—let's take each of the above fifteen typical miscalls above and briefly discuss what you *should* do instead:

1. The Withdrawn Student

Since he is not disturbing your teaching or the students' learning, during your class just let him be. If you are concerned about this student, make sure that you see him after class, or perhaps at an office hour; do not speak to him in front of the class. And, don't approach him with anger. Any kind of irritation in your tone would make the student defensive, argue with you, or have the student withdraw more. Instead, you need to do a slow, supportive, turn around ("screwdriver") approach.

You may want to ask him, "Tom, are you OK? I'm concerned about you. Do you think you'll be able to do well on the Midterm? I'm not angry with you. If I can help, let's talk." He'll probably say, "I'm fine." That's OK. Keep laying out a "red carpet" for him. Don't question him to death. Let him be, but let him know you care. If he opens up and says anything, immediately say, "I understand." Don't argue with him, even if he says, e.g., "College is a waste." This is not the time for a lecture on future careers. His feelings need to be listened to and not judged. Try to share: "I also felt that way sometimes." Perhaps you may learn more about why he is withdrawn in your course, or generally withdrawn. Then, you can decide if you can help, or perhaps refer him for further help.

2. The Overreacted-to Rule

Obviously, just don't overreact. If the, e.g., "food problem" interferes with your teaching or their learning, tell them that food that is noisy or distracting is not allowed in your class. You can warn someone regarding noisy food, and if not heeded, see them after class, or at an office hour. But do not start out with "No food at all in class!" You will then be involved in a very hard-to-enforce rule, definitions of "food," and impossible inspections and secret hidings.

3. The "I've Got to Win Their Feelings" Need

Again, you can't always win students' feelings, though ideally you would like to. When you cannot do the latter, do not grab for a "hammer." The student who does not feel like you want her to feel is an education problem, not a discipline problem. I don't want to diminish the problem of, e.g., wrong attitude. But a "hammer" does not help here.

You may wish to talk to her at an office hour. You can ask her if something is wrong, reason with her, etc. But, if she still shows boredom during your lectures, you may try again in your teaching to excite her interest. But if you can't, I know you'll feel badly (I understand). But try to not take her feelings personally.

4. The "I Need Their Attention" Syndrome

Just remind yourself that sometimes you don't need their attention or that sometimes you just can't get it. Or, something may be more important to them than what you are teaching. As long as they are not disrupting your teaching or others' learning, just keep going. Hopefully, this inattentive student will pass your test on Friday. If not, then his failing is the best motivation for paying more attention. Notice, one way to work on this problem is to not just give a Midterm, but, instead, perhaps a test/quiz more often, e.g., every few weeks.

5. The "My Ego Is Hurt" Reaction

Simply recognize that that is what is bothering you. That it is not your teaching that is being disrupted—you can keep going—nor is the rest of the class disrupted. Let it slide or talk to a friend after school to repair yourself. You must face it: students' reactions often will not enhance your ego.

6. "They're Interfering with My Getting My Teaching Plan Done" Reaction

If a student's questions or comments are really not disruptive to what you are teaching, and these may help get across what you are teaching, try to postpone your need to get what you planned done. As I said above, if you succeed in driving the train of your teaching from A to B but no one's on the train, you haven't really taught anything. Instead of getting angry and making this miscall, you can calmly, not angrily, tell the class your concern about their falling behind; that you're worried they may not do well on, e.g., a standardized test coming up. You can say, "Let's talk about this that Tom just brought up, but then let's try to cover this topic before we run out of time to cover."

. . . Or, you can assign what you didn't get done in class (perhaps show them your outline?) for homework, not as a punishment, but as a way to be able to discuss what Tom brought up.

7. Displaced Anger

Simply recognize that your irritation is really left over from elsewhere and that you are taking it out on the wrong people or student. Apologize, tell the class about the past annoyance, that you don't mean to be annoyed with them, and get rid this irritation, hopefully at the right person at the right time. Or talk to a friend about your irritation.

8. "I'm Tired of Trying to Be Understanding All the Time" Reaction

Recognize that it's your patience that is drained and the student doesn't deserve your frustrated tone. Apologize if you lose your patience, tell the student that it is a very fair question (if it is), and tell him or her, "Sorry for my tone; I'm just a little tired." Then muster more patience while you teach. Then, try to get a well deserved rest after school. (Of course, all teachers deserve more money, support, smaller classes, more respect, etc.)

9. The Mirror Effect

Try to notice that you are more annoyed with this one student than is called for. As explained above, s/he may remind you of you (or your friend or a family member). Instead, try to deliver only the communication that is appropriate to this situation at this time.

10. The "I Need to Control" Reaction

Again, you only need to control in order to teach, protect the learning of the rest of the class, and evaluate them. Try to let slide what is not within this broad jurisdiction. You will find that your class may seem less controlled (by you) but heed more of the actual controls you really need in order to be a good teacher.

11. The "Steam" for "Smoke" Mistake

As best you can, decide whether the class's behavior is "steam" or "smoke": if it's the former, you need to channel it, e.g., form debate teams and have a debate, assign an argumentative essay. If it's "smoke," warn the students to "cool it" and/or "See me at my office hour."

12. The Venting for Cursing Mistake

Review page 32 where I discussed this already. Of course, you have every right to teach them (if you have time) the best, or appropriate, language for venting, e.g., "damn!" may be better than "shit," or "shucks" even better yet, if you like. But, respect that they may have a different cultural background. "Jesus!" may offend you but not be a curse to them.

13. The Prejudicial Mistake

Recognize your prejudices and biases honestly. We all have them. I remember that I used to call on this cute kid very often, though others had their hands up first or deserved to be called on more. I realized it and modified my behavior accordingly. While changing your prejudices (that takes a long time), do the fair, appropriate, and professional behavior.

14. Holding a Grudge

If you have warned a student three times, and he violates your rule, follow through with what you warned with a consequence that you can enforce. If he then starts the same disruptive behavior again tomorrow, don't punish him at the first infraction. Start out with a "clean slate." If your rule says, "three warnings," follow it so you treat him as fairly as any student who violates the rule. If he has served his "first sentence" at the first test, don't hold a grudge and go after him at the outset. Instead, start with warning #1.

15. The Punishing the Education Problem Mistake

A student who doesn't do the readings or who is withdrawn is now (according to our definition) not a discipline problem. These are education problems. With these, you need to: inquire supportively about the causes; try to motivate the student; give more feedback-comments on their papers; give participation credit to those that deserve these, and less credit to those that do not—all in your grading system. Anger at such a student, especially in front of the entire class, doesn't educate.

Please do not misunderstand me. Some disruptions are NOT miscalls, and we shall discuss these soon. However, first locating these miscalls and handling them better will go a long way toward helping you improve your management of disruptions in general.

E. HANDLING MISCALLS BY STUDENT CATEGORY

Now, let's take a look at all those behaviors that I associated with certain subgroups of students that I described above. Are any of *those* behaviors miscalls? Yes. These behaviors, by student category below, seem to be "miscalls" and thereby need "screwdriver," rather than "hammer," methods.

F. HANDLING STUDENTS WHO

Ask you to repeat; come late; leave early; whisper; bring children to class; challenge; manipulate; blurt out; can't write; are disabled; and so on

1) "The Mountain Climbers"

a. Since these students are often bilingual, you may find them asking you to go slower, or repeat something again because they are having language difficulties.
b. Or, at times, they may whisper to a friend during a lecture or even pass notes to consult regarding translating your instructions or lecture.

OK, these are miscalls if handled with a "hammer." But what is the best "screwdriver" method to handle these?

You should overlook these behaviors, unless it begins to interfere with your teaching or other students' learning. If it does, you should not treat these behaviors with irritation, especially in front of the class. Again, you can ask them to sit toward the back of the room, help each other quietly, or they can be referred to remediation services, counselors, or tutors to get help with the notes, or see you after class, or at your office hours.
c. They may often need further instructions about a missed lecture or homework assignment because they couldn't attend class (or came late, or had to leave class early) due to their need to take care of a problem at their job, or with their family or children.

This kind of behavior should not be "disciplined," especially at the start of your class or during your class. If their coming to class late disrupts the class, keep a couple of empty seats ("late chairs") by the entrance door for them to sit in upon arrival. Do not talk to them as they enter. They can see you after class if need be, or at an office hour. If they have to leave class early, instruct them to take a seat at the back of the room and to leave as unnoticed and as quiet as possible. They should still be responsible for the homework and receive no leeway on tests. Your standards and requirements outlined clearly in your Course Syllabus should handle lateness and leaving early. (See chapter 5.)

d. **They may sometimes need to bring their young child to class with them because they cannot afford to get child care when the college is in session, especially when the public schools are not.**

You should advise the parent-student who brings his/her child to class that the child may stay as long as s/he does not disrupt the learning of the class or your teaching. (For example, the parent can bring a coloring book for the child.) However, if the child is distracting your teaching or the learning of the rest of the class, the parent-student should know that they will have to leave the class with the child. Students who need to bring their children to class must speak with you beforehand for this permission (this can be stated in your Course Syllabus). You should, of course, discourage this privilege, and only allow it (with this above contract understood), if necessary. The other students will appreciate this "contract," both for its permission and its limits. Then, enforce it. If the parent-student resists your enforcement, tell the class that you will have to stop teaching (for example, for a test that is coming up soon) until the parent leaves with the child. The latter will exert peer/class pressure on this parent.

2) "The Well-to-Do"

e. **They may rest securely on their emotional confidence, and not be shy to challenge you regarding your rules, grading policy, and your presentation of the subject matter—all with, often, great cognitive agility.**

You should be confident enough to use their reasoning (wrestling with you) as an opportunity to teach. And, your Course Syllabus should be clear enough and well thought out enough to not be bent by these students, who eye ambiguity at every opportunity. Of course, when their "wrestling" does detract from your teaching, it is no longer a miscall. Cut off this debate and ask them to see you after class about this, or you can discuss this at an office hour.

3) "The Game Players"

f. **These students may often greet you with subtle compliments or even do you favors, sometimes small, even unwanted.**

Tolerate these, but only take these for what they really are.

g. **They may "yes" you a lot, "thank you" a lot, to the point that you don't really know what the student is really thinking.**

The same as (f) above; perhaps, reassure them that they can give their true opinions without fear of any reprisals. Show them this by example: if a student gives a dissenting opinion, be very respectful and supportive of this point of view, even if it is "wrong." Students will notice that you do this and feel more comfortable offering their opinions.

h. They may try to figure out the answer you want to hear, rather than really go through any reasoning process. They may do this no matter how much you try to teach reasoning skills, or ask rhetorical questions wearing a "poker face."

Keep wearing a "poker face." Delay giving the answers. Play "devil's advocate" and encourage debate.

k. They will either show you resentment, or grave sadness (sulk) in order to move you.

Let them be angry or sulk. Don't allow yourself to be manipulated. Stick to the standards and requirements you set down in your Course Syllabus.

4) "The Immature"

m. They may often raise their hands and ask you to repeat something, or ask what seems like, from your point of view, to be an "unnecessary" question.

Try to have patience and don't make the student feel stupid. If the problem persists, see the student after class, or at your office hours (not as a reprimand) with support. See if you can get the student some extra help. But, do not allow this one "slow" student to require so much of your attention during class so as to hurt the general quality and momentum of your teaching.

n. They may often forget your instructions, or what you explained.

Do the same as above in (m).

o. Their reasoning may be swayed by emotion and/or be full of fallacies.

The same as above, but, also, try to concretize the reasoning as much as possible. Use lots of examples and visual aids, and write out the reasoning steps on the chalkboard whenever you can. (Use some of the methods described in chapter 6, below.)

p. They may not be able to explain, or answer "*why* questions," but only fall into giving examples—where they often believe that just one case proves their point.

Point out to the students that examples are not arguments, that one instance does not prove a general point. Teach critical thinking, some logic and the detection of fallacies, and make them practice explaining without examples (at least, at the beginning of their arguments).

q. They may be so shy that you cannot get them to respond in class. And, when they respond on paper, their writing approaches illiteracy.

Don't go after them, especially during the class. They need support. Be warm and approving of those that volunteer in your class, including those who give the wrong answer. Encourage the shy students, but don't force them to speak. Arrange a way for them to write to you privately—where you can give them compliments for their ideas, and ask them to mention this "excellent point" that they wrote out to you—in class. For their writing problems, do not use a red pen, do not overcorrect too much, and try to refer them for writing help. If their first language is not English, admit: "I could not write, e.g., Spanish well, and English is a very difficult language in many ways." You can also refer them to your college's remedial Writing Center; hopefully your college has one.

5) "The Learning Disabled"

r. These students may need you to repeat something because they have a hearing or cognitive processing impairment.

Allow them to sit up close: help them get the notes from other students.

s. Or they may be late because of a physical disability.

If you are sure the physical problem is real (a doctor's note?) allow them flexibility in your Course Syllabus' requirements—hopefully clearly stated. Also, the suggestions above in 1c may be appropriate. Hopefully, your college has support services for students with disabilities.

t. Or they may need more time to fulfill an assignment or take a test because of a writing or reading disability (though deceptively, they may have quite competent oral skills).

Here, you might require a doctor's note so that the other students feel it is fair to them to give more flexibility on time requirements. But, keep in mind, too much "forgiveness" does not build strength in the disabled. (On this point, I recommend that anyone who has not seen the movie Wait Until Dark should see it. A great movie and a great lesson.)

G. HANDLING MISCALLS REGARDLESS
OF STUDENT CATEGORY

Above, we have highlighted some potential miscalls per certain subgroups of students, and have discussed some possible "screwdriver" methods to handle these better. Now, what about behaviors *regardless of the student sub-group*: *A–L* above that were spelled out in chapter 1, section C? And what about the *extreme behaviors: M–V* mentioned in chapter 1, section D? Are any of these miscalls?

Let's take a closer look at E, J, K, and L.

E. Withdrawn, Inattentive, or Sleeping in Class, or Reading, or Doing Another Subject in Your Class

Are these behaviors disrupting the learning of the rest of the class and/or your ability to keep teaching? Sure, it bothers your ego, or may limit the learning of this one, e.g., sleeping student, but then it is still a miscall to go after such behaviors in front of the class. (However, if the sleeping student is *snoring*, then his/her behavior *is* disrupting your teaching and the learning of the rest of the class. This is *not* a miscall. Then see chapter 3, section G, p. 51.) Of course, if one, then three, then seven students start to do this, you should not go after them, but go after YOU. Your teaching is boring? They lack engagement methods? (For help with engagement methods, see chapter 6.)

A student is doing his Math homework in your History class? Is he really bothering others' learning? Can't you go on with your teaching? If your teaching really helps him pass the tests, then he will not do well on the tests. Or your teaching is irrelevant to him doing well on your test? Then, your teaching and/or tests need revision, not the student's behavior.

J. Inappropriate Demands for Your Time and Attention

This should not be handled with irritation. Instead, it should be handled by: asserting yourself; having scheduled office hours clearly stated and followed in your Course Syllabus; and by a philosophy of both "feeding and weaning." Let me elaborate.

You should not answer needs for individual help during your teaching that last more than a moment, as you will satisfy one student but derail your teaching for the rest of the class. Students who need help should be referred to either seeing you after class (not at the beginning of class), or referred to your office hours clearly stated in your Course Syllabus. You need to assert yourself here. And keep in mind that your helping a student is not helpful if you only *nurture* him; you should also wean this student to help him solve and work on problems by himself. Teach them how to "fish" rather than give them a "fish." If you easily feel guilty at weaning, keep in mind that your job is to grow knowledge and strength, not give passing grades and encourage dependence.

K. Poor Personal Hygiene (e.g., offensive body odor)

Again, this is obviously not something to discipline, especially in front of the class. This student needs some feedback delivered gently. Often, this feedback will come soon from someone else, hopefully someone who delivers it well. So, try to ignore it the first time. However, if it persists, see the person after class or at an office hour. Make sure there are no peers in earshot and say something like, "I want to be helpful; I think you need to take a shower. I know when I do not shower for a while, it can put people off."

L. Students Text Messaging Each Other During Your Teaching

Can you keep on teaching, aside from your personal reaction? Would you rather they do this "talking" orally? Of course not. Such behavior only affects these students who are texting; it does not interfere with the learning of the rest of the class. You can remind the whole class, for example, that next week there is a test on the topic that I am now going over, or remind these students after class or at an office hour. If your teaching matters, they will be affected then. To call attention to this texting during the class only makes *you* the most disruptive one in the class.

Now, a discerning reader may notice that though we have suggested better "screwdriver" methods for potential miscalls[2] per student subgroup and potential miscalls *regardless* of the student subgroup—we have *not* discussed how to handle those behaviors that are NOT miscalls: *i, j, l,* and *A, B, C, D, F, G, H, I,* and all the *extreme behaviors M—V*. We will now discuss how to handle *these*—in the next chapter.

NOTES

1. Gerald Weinstein and Mario Fantini, *Toward Humanistic Education* (New York: Praeger),1970.
2. In order to practice distinguishing miscalls from real discipline problems, and to work on your own typical miscalls, see chapter 9. For more help with miscalls, see Prof. Howard Seeman's *Preventing Classroom Discipline Problems*, 3rd edition.

Chapter Three

Handling Discipline Problems

A. In-Class Disruptions
B. Campus-wide Disruptions

To review: The behavior is NOT a miscall—instead, it is a discipline problem—if it needs to be handled immediately in class, and the behavior is (not merely the expression of a feeling) disrupting (or is potentially disruptive to) the learning of the rest of the class (not just the learning of the disrupter), or disrupting the role responsibilities of the teacher (not just the personal feelings of the teacher).

Thus, the following seem to be "discipline problems": *1.i; 2.j; 3.1; and A, B, C, D, F, G, H, I*, and all the extreme harmful/disruptive behaviors are *M–V*. What should we do about *these*? (We use the numbering code that we used for these behaviors in the previous chapters.)

A. IN-CLASS DISRUPTIONS

1. (i) Students who argue about their lateness, absence, or your grading with great excuses and sob stories to bolster whatever wrangling they can come up with to bend you.

Lateness

As I said earlier, you may want to save some empty seats near the entrance door to your classroom for latecomers to sit in when they arrive late. This will guard against these latecomers parading in front of you as you are teaching. Then, if the student comes to class late, but sits in a seat near the entrance to the class, then it would be a miscall to call attention to this student. Also, you may want to tell them that three lates = one absence.

Absence

You may want to inform students in your Course Syllabus that, e.g., three absences = a five pt. lowering of their grade, and that, e.g., three lates = one absence. And/or they are marked absent once they have come in late when you have already taken attendance. If they want the "absence" fixed to a "late" they must see you after class, not during the class. If they forget: they are/were marked absent.

Another method, if you do not want to call the roll at every class, you can pass around an attendance sheet that they must all sign. However, to guard against forgeries, at the first class have them all sign this attendance sheet. Then make many copies of it for the whole semester where they sign in next to their original signature, to see that it is authentically their signature. (You may want to warn that a forgery will, for example, go on their record. More on this in the Course Syllabus as a contract in chapter 5.)

Grading

The best way to stem these arguments, e.g., about your grading, is to have your grading system clearly spelled out and thought through in your Course Syllabus (see chapter 5). Nevertheless, try not to engage in such discussions either before or during your class. Always defer the student to see you after class or better: during your office hours. At that appropriate time, you should be able to refer them to the clear "contract" on these issues found in your Course Syllabus. If you have thought out your rules and standards there well, you should not deviate from these, without good, fair reasons. If you do deviate, keep in mind that you may incite the wrath of other students who will hear that you bowed to pressure from a student, and then you may have to see ten students during your office hours. Therefore, it is essential that you clearly state your limits and standards well (and if need be: clear exceptions) in your Course Syllabus. Then, be careful to keep track, be fair and consistent, and follow through.

If you do all the above, you will be able to cut off easily and prevent/handle most wrangling and manipulations regarding these above behaviors.

2. (j) Students who think you can be made to feel guilty will imply (or even state explicitly) that you are being racist, sexist, or just unfair. Some will even threaten you to go to the "the higher-ups" about the matter.

Of course, as with all of these behaviors, do not discuss these accusations in class; try to defer these discussions to an appointment at your office hours.

Then, if you are not guilty, try to stick to your standards and your judgments. Of course, this means that you have carefully made your judgments without bias. Assume that we are all diseased with societal prejudices somewhat— except for those who recognize how they have been brainwashed about these in their own upbringing, or those who have worked to rid these pollutions from their perceptions and opinions.

If you have not looked at yourself here, and are not careful here, you will judge students unfairly. It is incumbent upon all teachers (actually everyone!) to do this "work," to study your judgments and standards *before* you enter the classroom. You need to formulate fair criteria and rules and standards *before* you teach the class, and *before* you make up your Course Syllabus.

If you have done the above work on yourself, and are then confident about the fairness of your judgments, try not to bend to such accusations or threats. Spell out carefully your rules and grading system in your Course Syllabus as best as you can. (See chapter 5.) Then, try to keep careful records of your judgments, grades, and criteria for these with each student, e.g., copies of their papers or your comments. Try to give students early indications of poor work, that you can show them, or that you can, if need be, show to any "higher-ups" they may threaten to go to. If your administration is careful here, they have also keep records of students who have a "reputation" of these kinds of manipulations.

3. (1) Students who call out.

When students call out, they make the discussion a "race to the answer for approval." A good discussion, that teaches, e.g., critical thinking, is then disrupted by students calling out, questions or answers. Such also does not let you guide their learning nor help you steer how best to teach. Often teachers allow calling out because they are desperate for class participation. However, if you are, it is better to use "engagement methods" (see chapter 6) than settle for what is actually disruptive to good learning and teaching. To stem this disruptive behavior, a teacher needs to practice using certain guidelines for handling/curtailing calling out.

The best way to *nail down*—or should I say *screw down*—handling calling out is to watch the effective teacher vs. the ineffective teacher doing this here on a video that I made years ago. (In the video, that is me; only now I am a bit older.) The "students" in the scenes are real teachers who are role-playing disruptive students, *their* disruptive students who tend to call out. Most of them have problems with students calling out who are in high school, so they role-played those students. However, the video is still useful for understanding how to handle: *calling out.* For you, you can imagine not high school students (that is why I unfortunately use the term *kid* instead of *student* in the video) but your college students. However, the skills to curtail calling out that you will see in this video are very similar, regardless of the grade level.

The video is about five minutes long. Go to www.classroommanagement online.com/callingout. To view the video, you will be asked for a username; use PROFSEEMAN (all caps). You will also be asked for the password, which is 6666. You may have to enter these twice.

Now you can view the video demo on calling out. I hope the video is instructive.

Now, let me spell out what I just demonstrated in the video into several clear guidelines for handling *calling out*. Although it will take practice to retrain reactions, try these steps:

a. Don't call on the first person who raises his/her hand. This only encourages a "horse race" of who can give the answer first. Then, the slower ("losers"), but more thoughtful students, may just feel like withdrawing. So, instead, wait; nod your head in recognition as one hand comes up, two, three, etc. Wait till five or six think they know the answer. Then, call on someone. This will give them all time to think.

b. Only respond to students *who raise their hand*. And that means *don't* respond to a student who calls out as s/he raises her/his hand.

c. Go deaf, dumb, and blind to any questions, answers, comments that come without a hand raised, that you have not called on. Just don't hear his/her answer or see the student, even if s/he is the only person calling out the right answer.

d. Don't say to the call-outer, "John, stop it. I won't call on you." That is already giving John "negative attention." In a way, you have then called on him. Just ignore him, as if he doesn't exist, and call on a hand raiser (even if the hand raiser says the same thing John said).

e. Don't feel like you need to respond to every response. You can't feed all students all the time. After you get some responses, go on with your teaching.

   If you try to respond to every response, the train of your lesson will slow down to the point where students will "turn off" (get off) and withdraw.

f. While you go deaf, dumb, and blind to call-outers, give a lot of attention to the hand raisers: look at the person you call on; call him/her by name; write his or her answer on the chalkboard; perhaps, put his/her initial(s) next to the answer; thank him/her for the answer.

g. Meanwhile, keep aware of any students who were calling out who may try raising their hand to get the recognition you are giving out to the hand raisers. The second a former call-outer decides to "turn over a new leaf" call on him/her immediately to reward this new behavior.

h. If you feel you must say, "I won't call on anyone unless they raise their hand," don't say it to anyone or to the class. Say it as you're writing on the chalkboard, or say it looking at the floor. If you say it to the class, you may be giving "negative attention" to the call-outers.

These guidelines require practice. You are trying to train yourself to train the students for a more productive discussion where they do not step all over each student's contribution. Work at it. Catch yourself making the mistakes I've described above and persist. The class will come around if you're consistent about these guidelines. However, don't get starved for lack of class participation. Don't recognize someone who calls out just because no one else is participating.

You want class participation, but not calling out? See chapter 6 for many useful engagement methods.

(A) Students Who Do Not Respect Other Students' Opinions

Such should not be handled with a reprimand. Instead, the teacher needs to encourage respect for differing viewpoints. Perhaps, the teacher can sometimes require that a student must be able to give a summary of the last student's point before s/he can go on and give his/her own counter opinion. The last student, if s/he feels that the summary is satisfactory, can then say, "OK, you can now give your opinion." Only then can the next student respond.

Or you can teach them the difference between statements of fact and statements about feelings. The former can be argued about logically and respectfully.

The latter are not right or wrong but the person's feeling about the topic. If John thinks the movie was boring while Sue thinks it was great, they are both "correct."

(B) Students Who Monopolize the Discussion

If you have worked on the skills above to stem calling out (see 3 above), you can control who speaks when. Just make sure you give every student a fair turn. You can even have the last person who spoke call on the next person to speak. If a student goes on too long, ask the student: "John, so what is the point you are making?" Then thank him, and you (they) can move on.

(C) Students Who Talk While You or Another Student Is Talking

First, decide if this talking might be a "miscall." Can you let it slide? Is it really interfering with your teaching or is it only personally annoying? Only the latter? Then the latter indicates it may be a miscall to go after this behavior immediately in class. Is it really disturbing the rest of the class or is it just disturbing one student? If it is the latter, then you run the risk of YOU being the most disruptive to the learning of the class if you go after this behavior.

However, if you really think you cannot let this behavior slide, that this "talking" IS disrupting your teaching and/or their learning, then you need to have planned a set of warnings, each with consequences, that get more and more severe as the warnings escalate.

For example: At the first time the "talking" is disruptive, stop teaching and just give the talker a look. Second time, another look, with something like: "John, please." or "John, it is difficult for me to teach while you are talking; please . . . !" Third time, "John, please see me after class." (At the *see me after class* phrase, express your irritation about this, and do not engage in any arguments to the contrary.) Fourth time, again: "John, please see me after class." This time at the *see me after class* (or at an office hour) tell the student that if this behavior persists you will have to report his behavior, for example, to the Dean of students. If necessary, if this keeps happening, you can just stop teaching and say something like: "Class, if we do not cover all the material because I have to stop like this, you are still responsible for this material on the Midterm coming up soon." This statement will then exert peer pressure on talkative John.

(D) Students Who Constantly Ask Questions

Answer the first few questions. Be on the lookout if these are challenges. If they are, fine. Use your knowledge and logic and throw back questions to the student, if it can be a teachable moment. However, if these are not challenges, but a real lack of knowledge, answer the first few, then postpone this help to seeing the student after class or at an office hour.

(F) Students Who Eat in Class

Here again you must ask yourself if the eating in class is disrupting the other students' learning or your teaching. Can you continue to teach with John quietly eating a muffin in a seat in the back of the room? Yes, then, ignore it.

Is he crumpling wrapping paper around this muffin? Will this noise last more than five or ten seconds? If you call attention to him, will YOU be more disruptive to the moving train of your lesson than his eating? I am not saying what to do yet, I am telling you how to decide what to do so that you do not fall into a miscall.

However, if the food is ongoing, such as potato chips that make noise for minutes, then simply stop and first nonverbally signal that the noise is disruptive. It is always best to try a nonverbal signal first because it creates less embarrassment to an audience. If that does not do it, then say something like: "John, that noisy eating is disrupting my teaching. Please either eat with no noise at all, or please put it away. Thank you." On the other hand, if the class is almost over anyway, wait and speak to him after class, or if continuous and really necessary, at an office hour.

You may also tell the students at the beginning of the semester (or explain in your Course Syllabus) that they should make sure that they clean up after themselves and that if you find their seat dirty or you get complaints about food crumbs left at their seat, you will have to rescind the privilege. (Some colleges have college-wide classroom rules about eating in class; check yours.)

(G) Students Who Make Constant Noise (e.g., tapping a pen; sleeping and snoring)

Is this noise short lived as with the food situation above? Yes, then let it slide. You can't concentrate and keep teaching? It is disruptive to the rest of the class's learning? First just give the pen-tapper a look. This should do it. If not, then, stop and say something like: "John, sorry but that . . . is disrupting my teaching, distracting. . . . Please." It should not be necessary to see him after class or at an office hour. But, if you have to . . .

If the student is just sleeping, it is a miscall to go after him with anger in front of the class (see chapter 2, F.2.). However, if he is snoring, he *is* disrupting your teaching and the learning of the rest of the class; this is not a miscall. Then, let the class know, perhaps even with a smile, about your awareness of the snoring. Now you need to wake the snorer, but in the least embarrassing way, with the least audience reaction. Perhaps you can write a brief note like: "You are sleeping and *snoring*. See me after class." and tap him on the shoulder to gently wake him and give him the note, as you continue to walk around the room teaching. After class, since his sleeping is a miscall, do not show him anger, but, instead, concern about his passing the course or the test coming up.

(H) Students Who Come to Class Late or Leave Early

For lateness, see 1 above.

If a student needs to leave early, inform students (in your Course Syllabus; see chapter 5) that if they have to leave class early—to please take a seat in the back of the room, near the back door (or near the front door) so that they exit with as little disturbance as possible. They do not need to tell you the reasons for this, so do not try to create a fair system of "appropriate leavings." Instead, tell them that they are still responsible for all work in the course, and that you cannot figure their reasons for these leavings into their final grade. If you try to listen and judge excuses, you will be involved in a tiresome task that may only motivate better creative alibis, and accusation by others of you playing favorites.

(I) Students Who Use Pagers, Cell Phones, iPods in Class

As in the movies, instruct all students to turn off their cell phones, pagers, iPods in class and that they are not to be used during class. Warn them that disruptive use of these will warrant that they first see you after class and/or at an office hour, or may lead to, e.g. reduction of half a letter grade on a paper or a test. If you want to warn of confiscation, careful: it is best not to try to take away, e.g., a cell phone midst class; never try to take anything away from a student in front of his peers. Such pits the student against you for an "arm wrestle," or worse, where the student does not want to "lose face" in front of his/her peers. Subtracting points or a letter grade is easier than trying to enforce confiscation. If you want to do the latter, you had better plan how to confiscate the cell phone (always in private, e.g., at an office hour), for how long, and how/when to return it.

Have this policy clearly stated in your Course Syllabus. (See chapter 5.)

(M) Students Who Use Profanity and/or Pejorative Language

Profanity

Often, the best simple reaction to a curse word is: "Please!" However, you must distinguish between cursing vs. venting. If a student's, e.g. pen breaks and he mutters "Shit!" make no big deal about it, and keep teaching. If it is cursing at someone, e.g., "You are a shit!" and this starts into a verbal fight, warn them both that *both* need to stop this now. Do not get into who started it. If it persists, ask both of them to see you after class or at an office hour. There, you can ask them to take the "fight" outside of your class where they are not being disruptive to others' learning and your teaching. You may want to warn them: "I do not want to write this up."

If the curse is at *you*, do not arm wrestle them verbally for an apology in front of the class. Just say something like: "I will, for now, let that language go. I understand you are upset. We can discuss the matter at one of my office hours." Of course, revise these suggested statements to fit what is congruent for you. (See chapter 4 on congruence if need be.)

Pejorative Language

These include prejudicial judgments, "dissing" another student, putting down someone's feelings, values, or religion, or even, at times, sarcasm. You can show your displeasure with these kinds of comments. However, if they persist, you may want to spend some class time early in the semester on these issues. Some of the points you may want to make or teach are:

1. Stereotyping distorts and usually comes out of: first anxiety then anger. (Gordon Allport, *The Nature of Prejudice*.)
2. Feelings are not right or wrong; empirical descriptions of data are right or wrong. If I think the movie is great, and you think it was boring, we are both correct.
3. Values are chosen. We can study the consequences of value systems and cultures, but arguing is best done at judging the effect of the values. And these are best judged not from outside the culture.
4. Religions are belief systems as part of one's culture and needs regarding faith, dealing with ethics, mortality, etc. They do not often obtain their validity from facts, but from faith and tradition. It is best to respect the differences in religions at the time (unless your class is actually about this subject. Then, of course discuss it.)
5. Sarcasm often ridicules the opponent of an argument, and is often a clever, but non-logical, way of making a point. Help students to curtail the put-downs and discuss things with the use of reason. A successful put-down does not "win" an empirical, logical argument.

(N) Students Who Are High or Selling Drugs

This problem has become a serious one in many colleges. It is serious enough that often local law, or at least the college itself, dictates a rigorous policy to be followed by all staff. A new instructor needs to learn that policy first. Often, s/he is obligated to follow it.

However, I believe the best guidelines for such a policy are the following:

1. Distinguish between a student who is "high," a *user* (perhaps even a victim), and a student who is a *dealer*, who is selling drugs in the school (or school zone).
2. The user should be treated differently than the dealer.
3. Often, the *user* is withdrawn, falling asleep in class, red-eyed, and "out of it." The student needs help, not anger, nor for you to call the police. In this case, follow the guidelines for "withdrawn students" in chapter 2 F. 1. Try to see this student at an office hour and be supportive. Once you have gained a trusting relationship with the student, try to refer him/her for professional help. (See 18 below on how to best refer students for professional help.)
4. The *dealer* is different. S/he is a menace to other students. Often, the student may also be carrying a weapon. Unless you are sure you have the skills to warn and stop this person by yourself, you should not take him or her on yourself. It is best to confidentially report him or her to college security personnel and let these authorities approach this student according to their procedures. (Suggestions in 19 below may also be helpful here.)

(O) Students Who Are Verbally Abusive

Use the guidelines in M above.

(P) Students Who Harass Others

Use the guidelines in M above. If you want/need to stem bullying—a large issue to take on—you can get more help at these websites:

http://www.bbclic.com/
http://www.beatbullying.org/
http://www.bullies2buddies.com/

(Q) Students Who Cheat on Tests

This is a problem best not reprimanded during the test. To do so often creates more disturbance during the test, and, thereby, more opportunities for others to cheat. The best way to handle cheating is by *curtailing and preventing* it. I offer some tips here.

Tip 1

When you give a test, arrange students' desks in neat rows and sit in the back of the room. When students can't see you well, they are usually more nervous about trying to cheat. Those who are tempted to cheat usually will try to turn around to see where you are. That makes it easy for you to spot potential cheaters.

Tip 2

Cheating is easier when you give a short-answer test—for example, tests with true/false, fill-in-the-blank, or multiple-choice questions. Try instead to give tests that require short-essay responses. Yes, short-essay tests might be more difficult to *grade* than the others, but it actually takes more work to *design* valid and reliable short-answer questions that are not guessable.

Tip 3

If you still prefer short-answer tests, create two sets of tests. On one set, type the questions from 1 to 10; on the other set, arrange the questions in the opposite order. Copy one set of questions on white paper, and copy the other set on yellow paper. Pass out the two versions of the test to alternate rows of students; students in the first row get the white version, students in the second row get the yellow test, and so on. Tell the students you have done this so that if they are tempted to cheat, they'll be copying the wrong answer. Another good thing about setting up the test this way is that you can use one answer key to grade both sets of papers.

Tip 4

As I indicated above, don't take away the paper of a suspected cheater, or reprimand him or her in the middle of taking a test. Such an action will cause a disturbance during the test, and the disruption will give other students an opportunity to cheat. Instead, inform students before the test that, "If I suspect that anyone is cheating, I won't say anything during the test. If you get your paper back with points off, you'll know why." A statement such as that may often make potential cheaters too nervous to cheat.

Tip 5

Tell students at the start of the test, "During the test, cover up your answers." You might even let students know that any student who helps another cheat also will face repercussions. By encouraging students to cover up their own papers, you will probably be giving most students permission to do what they really want to do, since the ones that studied want deserved credit. By saying or directing this explicitly, these students will be more able to do this without risking peer disapproval. And, again, the students most likely to follow your "cover up" instruction are usually the ones who studied for the test, the ones who will have the most correct answers. In this way, you may cut off from view a major source of correct "cheatable" answers.

Tip 6

Don't wait for the day of the test to tell students how you'll handle cheating. By then, it's too late to motivate students to study, rather than to try to cheat. Instead, give warnings about cheating (that is, the tips you will follow) a day or two before the test. By doing that, you might motivate a potential cheater to study instead of risking cheating, especially when s/he hears the obstacles you have prepared by following the above tips.

Tip 7

Return test papers at the end of a class session—not at the start of a class session. Doing that is helpful in two ways:

- Students will be more likely to listen to a review of the test and your re-teaching certain points that were on the test *before* they get their papers back.
- If you return papers at the beginning of class, cheaters who lost points or got zeroes might vent their anger and disrupt your planned lesson. If they get back their papers at the end of the period, they can talk to you after class. Even better, they may go home to vent, and cool off by the time you see them the next day. They might even be motivated to do better on a future test.

Tip 8

Many colleges keep track of students accused of cheating by entering their names to a "clearinghouse," either on computer data, or by actually saving a copy of the test of the accused. If the student's name/tests appear, e.g., three times, the student can be put on probation or expelled from the college. By informing students of this policy, cheating can be curtailed, and other teachers, in other courses, can concur on this cheating behavior.

(R) Students who Plagiarize

Again, this is not best handled by "disciplining a student" in front of the class. It is best handled by giving back his/her paper with no grade at the top, but instead with: "See me at my office hours." Do not discuss this in front of the class or in class. Then, the way this is to be handled should be spelled out in your Course Syllabus. (See chapter 5.) Most colleges have a school-wide policy on plagiarism. Also, recently, there are many tools available, especially software and websites, to help teachers detect plagiarism. One example is Turnitin at global.turnitin.com. You can also just copy some suspected sentences into Google and hit search to see if the sentences appear in any already published documents that the student has not given credit to.

Many colleges keep track of students accused of plagiarism by entering their names to a "clearinghouse," either on computer data, or by actually saving a copy of the plagiarized paper of the accused. If the student's name appears, e.g., three times, the student can be put on probation or expelled from the college. By informing students of this policy, plagiarism can be curtailed, and other teachers, in other courses, can concur that this student tends to plagiarize.

B. CAMPUS-WIDE DISRUPTIONS

The rest of the disruptive behaviors listed below are not only disruptive to the class but can also be dangerous campus-wide.

(S) Students Who Threaten to Harm Themselves or Others

Again, such behavior should not be discussed or handled during your class. Instead, ask that the student see you after class or at an office hour.

If the student is threatening, e.g., suicide, your first stance should be to just listen. Allow the expression of self-anger, depression, loss . . . and do not try to argue with it. Logic usually has no leverage here, and is often construed as, "You don't understand." After showing understanding about these feelings and showing care, make an appointment to see the student again, soon—that is, if you think that the suicide is not imminent. Eventually, when you think he will go, refer this student to professional help.

Referring to professional help is an art. Follow these guidelines.

If you discover in your talks with the student that you neither have the time nor the skill to handle his problem, then you may need to refer him for some professional help. Again, *referring* is a skill. It can be done wrongly. Don't immediately say, "OK, you need to see a college counselor." The student usually will never go or may go with you once and never show up again. Instead:

1. allow the student to depend/lean on you for a while;
2. at the right time, after a few meetings, let the student know you want to help him but that you don't know how best to help, or that he deserves more time than you have;
3. tell him you know someone personally who can help him better;
4. tell him he's not alone, that many students have these problems and also see your "friend" for help;
5. go to the first counselor meeting with the student and help him present his problem;
6. however, prepare the counselor before you both arrive;
7. leave the first session only when the student feels comfortable;
8. encourage the student to keep going to the counselor;
9. let him see you if he feels uncomfortable with the counselor;
10. if this is not a good match, you need to start this process again as I explained above, until you find a counselor that is a "match";
11. hopefully, if the counselor is helpful, the student will "leave" you, not you leave him.

Here is an emergency help line for the prevention of suicide: 1-800-273-TALK (8255). If you feel that the student is making a credible threat against you or anyone else: report this as soon as you can to the Dean of Students or the Counselors at your college. Also, make a note of it for your records, what was said and the time and date. Do not try to handle it during the class. At the time of the threat, do not argue or threaten the student back. Try to just go passive and continue with your teaching. Show the student that you are making a note of this threat, then report it after class.

(T) Students Who Are Physically Violent or Carry Weapons

Physically Violent

Don't try to stop a fight that is already in progress by yourself. You can only hold one student, which only enrages him more and/or makes him more of a target. However, if you can grab and stop the aggressive one (not the passive one), you might be able to stop the fight. But, it is difficult to make such a judgment. It is always best to get help. If there are two professors present, you can both pull the students apart. Then, let campus security handle the situation.

If a student threatens you, use the suggestions in 18 above. If the student becomes violent, protect yourself without being aggressive back. (Try to remember you are not on the street, this is not a street fight where your pride is personally involved.) You can also help the rest of the class leave the situation. Then, again, get help as soon as possible. Call campus security. (You should always have this phone number handy or in your cell phone.)

As of the writing of this book, some 500 colleges in the United States are now trying to develop training for students and staff in case of the worst: a shooter on campus or in a class.

> Hundreds of colleges across the nation have purchased a training program that teaches professors and students not to take campus threats lying down but to fight back with any "improvised weapon," from a backpack to a laptop computer. The program—which includes a video showing a gunman opening fire in a packed classroom—urges them to be ready to respond to a shooter by taking advantage of the inherent strength in numbers."[1]

Carry Weapons

Follow these guidelines:

1. If you suspect or notice that a student is carrying a weapon (a drug dealer/seller may carry a weapon), *do not* confront the student, whether the student is alone or with peers.
2. Try *not* to let the student know that you suspect or know that s/he may be carrying a weapon.
3. Instead (unless there is an immediate danger or use of this weapon), wait, make note of the suspicion inconspicuously, and do not take action until the class is over, or the student has left your immediate presence.
4. Then, immediately, alert a security officer in your college with a description of the student and the weapon. (Or, call this national campus security hotline: 1-888-251-7959.)

Why the above guidelines are best:

a. If you confront the student alone or with peers present (especially in the case of the latter), you risk a confrontation to save face in front of his/her peers that may incite the student to use the weapon.
b. If the student suspects that you know that s/he has a weapon, s/he may be inclined to dispose of it before you are able to call a security officer and may target you as the person that ratted on him/her.

c. If you wait till the student is out of your presence, when a security officer *does* search the student, the student will have little idea of who called the officer. (Students who carry weapons are generally always worried about being fingered. Thus, without specific suspicion of *you*, the student may wonder if the rat is one of a dozen possible teachers or students.) Thereby, if you follow my guidelines above, your confidentiality and safety will not be compromised.
d. The security officer is usually trained in the law regarding search and seizure, safe-search procedures, self-defense, etc. You are probably not. A mistake, and you not only risk violation of the law (therefore the inability to properly prosecute the incident), but risk your own and other students' safety.
e. Colleges are now required by federal law to "immediately notify" their students and staff upon confirmation of a significant emergency on campus, such as an active shooter situation.[2]

Unfortunately, there is a debate going on in many legislatures: *Should a student who has a license to carry a gun be allowed on campus with this concealed weapon?* Some actually think that a campus becomes safer when a student can carry a licensed concealed weapon on campus. But, do we actually make college campuses safer by allowing more guns?! What about the fear that one of those "law-abiding citizens," particularly a college student under the influence of drugs or alcohol, commits a crime because they have said weapon? It is not unheard of that someone gets injured while inebriated, but introducing a weapon in the matter can only make it worse.[3]

The argument goes: a law-abiding citizen with a gun will be faster to react and more likely to protect themselves and others against a shooter on campus as opposed to one who is not armed. But, this is an NRA argument. Whereas the author of this book believes that it is access to weapons that is the killer! As in the Old West: if the town is made safe (by the town marshal) e.g., college procedures and security officers, there is no need to carry weapons, and there are less killings. We need to work on methods for greater campus security; arming students on campus would only do more harm than any good safety.

As of April 3, 2008, only three universities in the United States allow students to have licensed firearms on campus, the names of which I am not permitted to publish.[4]

Parents who have become aware of this permissive policy often remove their children from these colleges. Instead, almost all colleges in the United States have these kinds of policies: *"A permit to carry a firearm, regardless by who issued, does not supersede [this college's] policy."*

Normally, the possession of weapons, firearms and/or ammunition is prohibited on any University of ＿＿ campus. Possession of a valid concealed weapons permit authorized by the State of ＿＿ is NOT an exemption under this policy. This policy, however, does not deny possession of firearms and ammunition by duly authorized law enforcement officials when such possession is unavoidable.

The introduction of guns, knives, or other such devices on campus is potentially dangerous to the entire ＿＿ community and inconsistent with a safe learning environment. Faculty, staff, and students are, therefore, advised that the introduction of any weapon is a direct violation of policy and a serious breach of security that will require immediate discipline, up to and including dismissal.

It is a serious violation of the law to possess a firearm or certain knives on District and college property. Section 626.9 of the *State of* ＿＿＿＿Penal Code makes it a felony to bring or to possess a firearm or certain knives on the grounds or within buildings of the ＿＿＿college campuses without the written permission of the president of the college or his/her designee.[5]

(U) Students Who Commit Sexual Assault/Raped

College students are more likely to be sexually assaulted than any other age group; in fact, four times more likely![6]

The best way to prevent and handle these crimes is through the power of information, backed up by campus diligence and support. Students need to be informed about this danger (both men and women) as well as the teaching faculty, counselors, and the college's administration.

A professor can help disseminate useful information about this crime to his/her students, such as at the beginning of classes, periodically throughout the semester, and on the classroom bulletin boards.

However, *all* members of the college community need to become informed about:

1. The procedures to follow after a rape has occurred, in order to successfully prosecute the offender;
2. The best precautionary behaviors to prevent becoming a victim of sexual assault/rape;
3. The crime of acquaintance/date rape;
4. What things a faculty member or administrator can do to curtail these crimes.

Although both men and women can be victims of rape, since the vast majority of victims are women, I will follow this generalization in my gender descriptions below.

1) Acquaintance/date rape

In the crime of acquaintance/date rape, the victim knows the rapist; she may even have been dating him.

Guidelines for Women

1. Trust your feelings if you feel that you are in a situation that does not feel safe.
2. Try to think out your own sexual limits before, e.g. starting to "make out." How far do you really want to go with the person you are with?
3. Be careful: being passive may seem like "a red carpet" to some and can encourage sexual aggression.
4. Be aware of any lack of respect when you try to assert your anger and limits.
5. You can test: Do you get respect when you say "no"?
6. Do not allow forceful behavior.
7. Remember that alcohol and/or drugs are involved in a large percentage of acquaintance rapes, and can affect your judgment.
8. Choose your date with an eye toward whether this person is an honest person, not with just an eye, e.g., toward whether he is attractive.
9. Let your friends know where you will be on your dates, and who you are dating. If possible, at first, double date with another woman friend, at least until you are more sure you can trust your date.
10. Do not accept any arguments that accuse you, the victim, of being the "culprit," e.g., dressing attractively should not be blamed for the motivation of these crimes.

Guidelines for Men

1. Respect sexual boundaries.
2. Do not objectify the person as a physical object. See them as people with feelings.
3. Pay attention to your date's body language as well as to what s/he is saying (e.g., if s/he stiffens up, s/he is probably not comfortable with how far you are going).
4. Be self-aware. Know when you are starting to cross the line, and are becoming "guilty."
5. Even if you have always believed that women sometimes say "no" when they mean "yes," always act as if "no" means "no."
6. It's never OK to force yourself on a woman, even if you think that she has been teasing and leading you on.

7. Remember that alcohol and/or drugs are involved in the majority of acquaintance rape, and affect your judgment.
8. Support women you date in being assertive and honest.[7]

2) Precautionary behaviors for all

1. Get to know your surroundings before you go out, and learn a well-lit route for going to and from your residence.
2. Always carry emergency cash and keep phone numbers for local cab companies handy.
3. Form a buddy system with close friends and agree on a secret "please butt in" signal for uncomfortable situations.
4. Trust your instincts. If you feel unsafe in any situation, go with your gut.
5. Avoid being alone or isolated with someone you don't know and trust.
6. Don't accept drinks from people you don't know or trust.
7. Watch your consumption of alcoholic beverages, especially when other people are drinking.
8. Do not accept drinks from an open container.
9. Never leave your drink unattended.
10. Buy bar drinks in bottles, if possible, because they are harder to tamper with than wide-mouth glasses.
11. Never leave your drink unattended; if you do lose sight of it, get a new one.
12. Always watch your drink being prepared.
13. Try to buy drinks in bottles, which are harder to tamper with than cups or glasses.
14. Avoid putting music headphones in both ears so that you can be more aware of your surroundings, especially if you are walking alone.
15. Learn some self-defense martial arts methods that can ward off an attack.
16. Know where there are "safe havens" where you are going in case you need to go to one, to get help.

3) Procedures to follow after a rape

- Do not shower, bathe, wash, douche, or attempt to clean yourself.
- Do not change your clothes.
- Do not urinate, as traces of drugs can be found in urine.

- If you drank from a glass or can, take it with you.
- If you can, also try to obtain the offender's glass.[8]

4) What faculty members or administrators can do to prevent attacks

1. Within the rights of the First Amendment, try to curtail sexual jokes and pornography that approve of violence.
2. Heed the concern of any student who says s/he is afraid of someone.
3. If your college unusually does not have them, help set up support services on your campus for both counseling potential predators and victims.
4. Urge students often, by using all kinds of media in many campus venues, to report any and all sexual assaults.
5. Publicize this emergency/information phone number and website throughout your campus:

   National Sexual Assault Hotlines:
   800-656-HOPE and rainn.org

   The caller's phone number or email is not retained, so the communication is anonymous and confidential.
6. Title IX of the Education Amendments of 1972, a federal law, requires that once a college knows, or reasonably should know, of possible sexual harassment of students, it must take "immediate and appropriate steps to investigate or otherwise determine what occurred and take prompt and effective steps reasonably calculated to end any harassment, eliminate a hostile environment if one has been created, and prevent harassment from occurring again" regardless of whether the student who has been harassed complains of the harassment or asks the college to act. When a college fails to do so, it becomes subject to legal action through the U.S. Department of Education's Office for Civil Rights.
7. Policies. Many universities across the United States have established legal/written policies regarding sexual assaults on their campuses. Students Active for Ending Rape (SAFER) compiles a College Sexual Assault Policies Database. This online database archives sexual assault policies from colleges and universities across the nation. Developed in response to student requests for examples of thorough and effective campus sexual assault policies, the database gives administrators and students access to policies from a diverse array of American universities. The database, funded in part by a grant from the American Association of University Women, can be found by visiting SAFER's website at: http://www.safercampus.org/policies.php.

SAFER offers basic guidelines for effective policies:

a. All students should have access to the policy;
b. The policy should be easy to understand;
c. Policies should be created with student input and formal oversight;
d. All policies should include mandatory prevention education for all students, crisis intervention, and long-term counseling;
e. Additional markers of a strong school sexual assault policy include a full-time staff person dedicated to the issue and the on-campus availability of contraception and STD prophylaxis.

8. Finally, a college can sponsor conferences and workshops on responsible sex education. Such can be done at a weekend, at a two day event, similar to the one in table 3.1.

Sexpertise is a two-day event that brings in local experts in the fields of sexual health and relationships for open, honest conversations and activities that give students the chance to ask these hard questions and have a little fun in the process!

Table 3.1. Sample of Conference Schedule

Time/Location	Event
Thursday, January 29, 2009	
1–2 p.m. **Terrace**	**Sexercise: A Survey of Human Sexuality** *Presented by: Bisexuals, Gays, Lesbians, and Allies in Medicine* All participants fill out a survey, then do an activity around human sexuality using a survey that isn't theirs.
2:30–4 p.m. **Terrace**	**Healthy Relationships Workshop/Panel** This event will answer your questions about healthy relationships— how to find one, how to stay in one, and how to communicate with your partner about what you need from a relationship.
4:30–6 p.m. **Terrace**	**Sexual Health Peer Educator Workshop** *Presented by: UHS Sexual Health Peer Educators* Your peers will present an interactive workshop around issues vitally important to your sexual health. This is the first of many events for this new, premiere sexual health group on campus!
6–7:30 p.m. **Terrace**	**PULSE Workshop** *Presented by: PULSE students* The PULSE representatives from your halls and houses are putting together a workshop to educate you on your sexual health and relationships.

(*continued*)

Table 3.1. (*continued*)

Time/Location	Event
3:30–5 p.m. Colloquium Rm 4448	**Sex, Drugs, and Alcohol** This multimedia workshop will invite participants to discuss the role alcohol plays when making decisions about intimacy and sexual involvement. Issues of media influence and campus culture will be included.
4:30–6 p.m. Rm 3048	**The Naked Truth** *Presented by: Pure Romance* Pure Romance and The Naked Truth answer your questions about sexuality, sexual health, and relationships. We also provide students with resources and information about sexuality and sexual health. This presentation is a lot of fun and a must-see!
6–7:30 p.m. Rm 3048	**Women's Empowerment Workshop** This workshop will explore strategies and options available to women in responding to and defending against sexual harassment and sexual violence. We will discuss three broad areas: awareness, assertiveness, and physical self-defense techniques.
8:00 p.m. East Quad Auditorium	**CAUTION: This Is How It's Caught** *Presented by: Matrix Theater* More info at: http://www.uhs.umich.edu/sexpertise/matrix.pdf.

Friday, January 30, 2009

Time/Location	Event
1–3 p.m. Terrace	**What's Friendship Got to Do With It?** This workshop will explore the current science of compulsivity and addiction as it relates to cyber relationships and exploring the impact it has on our own self-esteem, social skills, and abilities to build real, intimate relationships with others, as well as the impact on our day-to-day and face-to-face relationships.
12–1:30 p.m. Colloquium Rm 4448	**The HPV Panel** This panel will answer your questions about HPV—how it is transmitted, vaccinations and treatment ,and what the risks are.
4–5:30 p.m. Rm 3048	**Men's Health Panel** A chance for men to come together and discuss issues and concerns surrounding their sexual health.
4–5:30 p.m. Colloquium Rm 4448	**Women's Health Panel** A chance for women to come together and discuss issues and concerns surrounding their sexual health.
5:30–6 p.m. Colloquium Rm 4448	**Our Health Together** The men's and women's health panels come together to discuss issues relevant to everyone.
6–7:30 p.m. Rm 3048	**Sexuality and Persons with Disabilities** This workshop will help dispel some of the myths surrounding sexuality and disability.

*University Health Service, University of Michigan, Ann Arbor, January 29–30, 2009.

You should attend if you are:

- Sexually active
- A virgin
- Thinking about starting a relationship
- Just "hooking up" with someone
- Thinking about sex — right now
- Curious about your body
- Wondering the best way to date on campus
- Using contraception and want to learn how to use it better
- Interested in pleasure, intimacy, and connection

(V) Students Who Participate in Binge Drinking

College presidents agree that binge drinking is the most serious problem on campus. One study (Harvard University's School of Public Health) found that during a two-week period 44 percent of U.S. college students engaged in binge drinking. Even more disturbing, over half the binge drinkers binged three or more times in a two-week period.[9] And, the percentage of students who were binge drinkers was nearly uniform from freshman to senior year, even though students under twenty-one are prohibited from purchasing alcohol.[10]

Binge drinkers are dangerous to themselves and others.

What Can Each Individual Professor Do?

A professor can help disseminate useful information (see below) about this problem to his/her students, such as at the beginning of classes, periodically throughout the semester, and on the classroom bulletin boards.

What Can Be Done College-wide?

- Individual students almost always believe that most others on campus drink more heavily than they do; also, the disparity between the perceived and the actual behaviors tends to be quite large. In short, they do not realize the seriousness and the consequences of their own drinking. Therefore, by conducting surveys of actual student behavior and publicizing the results, the extent of heavy drinking is often significantly reduced.[11] Also, students should be informed that college-age students who drink heavily may increase their risk for future heart disease.[12]
- In freshman orientation sessions students can not only learn the facts about binge drinking (above) but also can be taught ways to reduce/handle stress

and how to plan ahead of time (with a "buddy") how much to drink before attending a social event, and who will be the designated driver.

- The college can also: offer social, recreational, extracurricular, and public service options that do not include alcohol and other drugs; limit alcohol availability; restrict marketing and promotion of alcoholic beverages; and enforce all campus policies with consequences for these behaviors.[13]
- In and around the college's campus, the college's administration can lobby local officials to: increase the penalties for illegal sales/services to minors; prohibit "happy hours" and other reduced-price alcohol promotions; and restrict hours of sales of alcohol.[14]
- Many experts agree that lowering the legal age (a proposal of many college presidents) won't fix a college culture that accepts binge drinking as the norm. (CBS Online News, Nov. 4, 2008). As a matter of fact, many believe that it would only make the practice legal at an earlier age and would do little to curtail it.
- Instead, college should heed the above suggestions, and its instructional staff should advertise often and prominently throughout its campus and classes the information that is readily available from the National Institute on Alcohol Abuse and Alcoholism (NIAAA), especially at: http://www .collegedrinkingprevention.gov/

For practice in handling some of the above situations in this chapter, the reader should see the exercises and checklist in chapter 9.

NOTES

1. Alan Scher Zagier, Associated Press Writer, "Colleges Confront Shootings with Survival Training," Aug. 26, 2008, http://www.usatoday.com/news/nation/2008-08-26-Colleges-survival_N.htm.

2. R. 4040, H.R. 4137, and H.R. 6432 Law, August 2008.

3. Stacey Talarovich, "Concealed Weapons on College Campuses?" *U. Town*, April 3, 2008.

4. Talarovich, "Concealed Weapons."

5. Summary statement of "National Survey of Campus Gun Possession Policies," January, 2009.

6. Rape, Abuse and Incest National Network, http://www.rainn.org/get-information, 10/08.

7. Many guidelines above suggested by the article: "Date/Acquaintance Rape Prevention for Him and Her," Connie Saindon, 1997, in *Self Help Magazine* at: www .selfhelpmagazine.com/index.php.

8. Rape, Abuse and Incest National Network.

9. Frequent binge drinkers were 21 times more likely to miss classes, damage property, get physically hurt, have unplanned/unprotected sex, get in trouble with police, and drink and drive.

10. Center for the Science in the Public Interest, http://www.cspinet.org/booze/collfact1.htm, 11/09.

11. Researchers reported on April, 25, 2007 at the American Heart Association's 8th Annual Conference on Arteriosclerosis, Thrombosis, and Vascular Biology.

12. H. W. Perkins, "College Student Misperceptions of Alcohol and Other Drug Norms among Peers," *The Higher Education Center for Alcohol and Other Drug Prevention* (1997), 177–206.

13. National Institute on Alcohol Abuse and Alcoholism (NIAAA) Task Force on College Drinking, July 11, 2007.

14. NIAAA Task Force.

Part Two

PREVENTING COLLEGE DISRUPTIVE BEHAVIORS

All of these examined strategies will help you better handle college disruptive behaviors. However, the best time to fix a problem is before it starts. We will now discuss college classroom/campus management in such a way as to work on preventing these disruptions from happening in the first place. We will focus on these areas in order to work on prevention:

Chapter Four

Being Congruent

A. What Is *Being Congruent*?
B. Online Video Demonstration on Congruence
C. Your Self-Presentation
D. Your Course Rules/Procedures
E. Congruent Delivery/Teaching Methods

Students are more disruptive to a teacher when they feel an "enemy" relationship with that teacher, when they feel that the teacher is not "for them," or is on the other side of the "fence." Conversely, if students feel that the teacher is "for them," is "with them," allied in helping them, students tend to work with this teacher and be less disruptive.

One way to form this "allied" relationship with students is by "being congruent" to them, and with them.

A. WHAT IS *BEING CONGRUENT*?

In short, though stating it simply, "being congruent" is being authentic, or not being phony. However, we need to elaborate here.

Carl Rogers uses the term "congruence" to describe a situation in which one's words, gestures, and behavior accurately reflect or correspond to what one is actually feeling.

If a speaker's words, gestures, and behavior do *not* correspond to what s/he is really feeling, then they are being "incongruent." What Rogers calls being incongruent our students often call being phony, or "bullshitting." Students, most people, dislike phonies.

Let's take a closer look at exactly what this ability, being congruent, is for a teacher. All communicated messages (subject matter lectures, teacher's explanations, questions to the class) have a cognitive content delivered with an underlying emotional feeling; they, in a way, look like figure 4.1.

For example, if a teacher says in a History course, "Now class, we must look at the causes of this war." The MESSAGE looks something like figure 4.2.

When the message's top and bottom parts back each other up, or correspond (as it does in figure 4.2) the message is congruent. When the bottom of the message does not back up or correspond to the top, the message is incongruent.

For instance, "I am very glad you are here." See the incongruent message in figure 4.3.

Teachers may often deliver subject content, descriptions, rules, etc. incongruently. Students may notice at times that teachers are not really "behind" what they are saying. For example, a teacher who says in a monotone while yawning, "This topic is very important; the first important point is . . ."appears incongruent.

Another way to explain an incongruent teacher message, where the teacher, as person, doesn't seem to be behind what he's saying is to picture it like this:

TEACHER! / person

Here, the teacher's role is up front and the teacher as *person* is behind a mask, or a defensive posture. What the teacher says doesn't seem to be related to how he really feels as a person. The above teacher probably comes off incongruently to his students, whereas a *teacherperson* comes off congruently. The latter teacher is not trying to play the role of a teacher, but instead,

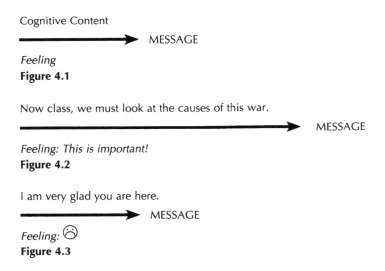

Cognitive Content

⟶ MESSAGE

Feeling

Figure 4.1

Now class, we must look at the causes of this war.

⟶ MESSAGE

Feeling: This is important!

Figure 4.2

I am very glad you are here.

⟶ MESSAGE

Feeling: ☹

Figure 4.3

is teaching how he teaches, his style; he is being himself while teaching such that who he is as a person is related directly to how he is as a teacher. He is not only not hiding his personality as he teaches but using it to reinforce his job as teacher. This teacher is congruent. One more way to picture congruence and incongruence might be to say that:

- A congruent teacher speaks from the heart, his/her true feelings.
- An incongruent teacher formulates messages from what he thinks will look good, or sound good, or from his or her image of what a teacher should look like or do, as if from a tape recorder in his head.

In summary, being incongruent looks phony to students, annoys them, destroys any ally relationship they feel with you, and becomes a potential source of, even motivation for, disruptive behavior. Teachers must endeavor to be congruent as much as possible, and in three main areas: Your Self-Presentation; Your Course Rules/Procedures; Your Teaching Delivery.

B. ONLINE VIDEO DEMONSTRATION ON CONGRUENCE

Perhaps the best way to *screw down* what congruence is might best be done by watching a demo about congruence. (In this video, that is me; only now I am a bit older.) My examples at the time were geared more toward high school students; that is why I inappropriately use the term *kids* rather than *students*. However, this skill—being congruent—is equally applicable to college students, and even to our personal social life in general. So, revise what you see here to fit your situation.

The video is about six-and-a-half minutes long. To view this video, go to www.classroommanagementonline.com/congruence. You will be asked for a username. Put in PROFSEEMAN (all caps). You will also be asked for the password, which is 6666. You may have to enter these twice. Now you can view the video Demo on Being Congruent.

I hope that the video further helped you understand what "being congruent" is.

Now, a little more details about this skill of "being congruent":

C. YOUR SELF-PRESENTATION

You need to try to be yourself, as much as possible, while you are teaching. Do not try to be "the teacher," be yourself. On the other hand, an *in*congruent teacher formulates messages from what s/he thinks will look good, or sound good, or from his/her image of what a teacher should look like or do. Whereas a *congruent* teacher delivers messages from who s/he really is, how s/he really feels, "from the heart."

Do not misunderstand what being congruent is. Acting is *not* being congruent. Actors take scripts written by others and then try to reinforce these lines with acted out, directed feelings. Sometimes they are effective with an audience, sometimes not. They are effective when their messages *seem* as if they are being congruent. But congruent teachers are not good actors. Instead, they first figure out what they are feeling, who they *are* with each message and interaction, and then articulate a message that truly matches what they feel. Learning to be congruent requires the ability to figure out or know your feelings, and then to formulate a content statement that comes out of, matches, how you really feel. Or, being congruent is not trying to be the kind of person a teacher is supposed to be. Instead, to be a congruent teacher is to be yourself while teaching, not to hide yourself while teaching; it is putting your real self into your teaching. The best way to work at being congruent is to keep trying to be yourself while teaching. Don't try to be "the teacher." Be a *teacherperson*.

In order to do this, you need to know yourself. You need to know how you feel about things. Hopefully, you are yourself at a party when someone asks you, "Do you want a drink?" and you answer how you really feel. If you answer how you should answer, or how one should be, you've lost your congruence.

To generally interact congruently with the class, you need to feel who you are and be comfortable being who you are. That means you need to check with yourself by asking, e.g., "Do I really feel that that student remark was funny?" "How do I feel about this subject matter that I am teaching and how can I best get this across?" "How do I feel about the rule concerning . . . ?" "How can I best formulate and follow through about this rule so that I am congruent with it, believe in what I am enforcing?"

It is not easy to be congruent. Why is it so difficult?

First, most of us do not bother to learn what it is we feel about things. We generally say we feel "OK," or "Fair," or "Not so good." But we seldom take time out to find out if we are feeling angry, guilty, sad, excited, bored, hypocritical about a rule, not sure why this particular thing is important, etc. We sometimes take time to study our feelings when: we write a diary, see a counselor, we try to figure out whether to have a baby or whether we should marry someone, etc. We feel these situations require a careful understanding of our feelings. Well, being a congruent teacher also requires that we learn to incorporate our real feelings into our teaching.

We also have trouble being congruent because we tend to teach the way we were taught, especially when we're anxious or don't know what to do. "I'll just be like Prof. Johnson, my old History teacher." Or, "I'll say what he would say here." Or, "I'll use the same Course Syllabus he gave me when I was a student." The problem here is that you have a different personality than, e.g., Prof. Johnson. What worked for him, what seemed real and honest when he did it, won't necessarily be so for you. And, if it's not congruent with you, it will not form an allied relationship with your students.

Also, anxiety makes us blind and more dependent. When we are anxious, we can't bother to see or can't see what we really feel. So we instead tend to quote, e.g., some strong person in our head. Be careful; you will most often be incongruent when you're anxious, worried, or nervous. At these times, slow down, resist trying to act like "the teacher."

Here are some ways to put more of your *person* into your teaching:

- Joke with them sometimes.
- Admit some mistakes, or problems.
- Use your own down-to-earth words, as much as you can.
- Tell them sometimes how you feel about some rules and topics you are teaching.
- Call them by their first names.
- Sometimes tell them how you're feeling today as you start teaching.
- Pat them on the back or shoulder, if you feel it as they are near you.
- Don't be afraid to smile, or wave "hello" in the hall, or after school.
- Share a personal story (especially if it relates to the topic).

I am recommending you allow your students to see at least some of your feelings—not only because congruence is effective and a preventative to disruption but also because their "radar" can tell how you are feeling anyway. So you might as well show them.

There are some difficulties that must be managed if you are to be more open with students. It is not just *being congruent* that is difficult. It is also often a delicate matter to manage the implications of such a policy. If a student asks you how you personally feel about some, e.g., political fact in your History class, by sharing your personal feeling you might influence him or her too much. Or, you might cut off their own responsibility for learning critical thinking or their own value clarification. In such cases, you might simply say, "I have a particular feeling about this. But, you need to decide here for yourself." "So, let me ask you. . . . " Also, sometimes it feels "uncomfortable," or "this is too private" to be fully congruent. But, you can say that, "I'd rather not discuss that; that is a personal issue." But, since this is accurately how you feel, you *are* being congruent.

One more clarification about being congruent here: I am not saying that being congruent is being "a nice guy." If you feel like being a nice guy, fine, be that way. However, if a student irritates you (and it's not a miscall), don't be a nice guy. Instead, express your appropriate irritation. You can also be congruent, *and be stern, and systematic*, when you really feel that you need to be.

D. YOUR COURSE RULES/PROCEDURES

Besides how you come off as *teacherperson* to your students, you also need to make sure that your rules and procedures for your course are congruent with your real beliefs. You will be delivering your: grading policy, late policies, standards of participating in your class, how students are responsible for homework, term papers, attendance . . . all via your initial Course Syllabus, and then often orally and in writing during your course. It is important that all these are well thought out and congruent with how you really feel about each policy—so that they be enforced consistently. If they are not, you will invite disruptive behavior.

Be careful: the rules/procedures that you decide to enforce need to be *your* rules, not those suggested by another teacher, or just out of a book. If they are from any of these, you'll need to decide if you can really *own* these "as is," or with revisions, or not at all. To the extent you can "get behind" the rules/procedures that you specify, to that extent they will be felt as yours and carry weight and thereby be less open to student manipulation. You need to think out how you feel about, e.g. your grading policy, extra credit, lateness, etc. Yes, you need to think out how you feel about these and what you will do, and can do—all *beforehand*, not on the spot. You not only need to know what you really feel like doing so you can act, but you also will need to plan this all out in your Course Syllabus. (We will in chapter 5.)

I wish it were the case that I could simply give you twelve or twenty policies that work. I can't. Your rules and grading policies need to be out of how *you* feel about each, come from who you are. All I can do is urge you to think them out now. Stop here and ask yourself: how do you feel about each of the following? And how would you follow through regarding these:

1. Absences
2. Lateness
3. Extra credit

4. Class participation
5. Your grading policy
6. Term papers and formatting
7. Cheating
8. Chewing gum
9. Being high in class
10. Cell phones
11. Eating in class
12. Unreadable handwriting
13. Students who don't do the homework
14. Note passing
15. Talking to another student while you're teaching
16. Calling out

Of course, you can use the guidelines in the previous chapter for handling many of these. You can also use the index of disruptive behaviors and solutions at the end of this book. But, you must make sure that in spelling out your rules/policies for these that you are congruent with all of them in both your Course Syllabus and what you consistently enforce during your course.

Keep in mind that you may have *mixed feelings* about, e.g., late homework, or note passing. If you do, say your mixed feelings in just a more complex policy. For instance, "I don't want to see late homework. I'll penalize you one point on your final grade for each late homework submitted. You can make up the homework, but only for that week. If you want to make up homework back two weeks, it's too late!" In other words, don't state a simple rule, if you don't feel a simple one way about it. But don't avoid figuring out the complex rule you feel congruent with because you have complex feelings about it. It's work to figure these out, but it'll pay off because your policies will be less apt to invite disruption during the whole semester.

E. CONGRUENT DELIVERY/TEACHING METHODS

You must deliver your subject matter in your teaching and lectures congruently. Especially in colleges where the content *is* the course, if you do not love your subject matter, it shows. If you do love it, your love will often be contagious. Students who feel that even the teacher doesn't care about the topic being taught not only turn off to that topic but also begin to resent that teacher. We must work on being congruent with the subjects we teach, or our incongruent delivery of the topic will be another source of eventual disruptive behavior.

Hopefully, you really do care about the subject you teach. Hopefully, you chose this subject as your major in college because you believe in its value. If you chose your major because you just liked Prof. Johnson (who just happened to teach History), but you really don't care for History, you're in trouble. You can't motivate a class about something you yourself are not motivated about. You can, maybe, fake it for a while. But, eventually you'll either burn out from faking your enthusiasm all day, all semester, or the students will sense your inauthenticity and eventually get irritated with you for "making" them take notes on all this "boring stuff."

Hopefully, e.g., at least 80 percent of the subject matter you do care about, do feel is valuable, but not some 20 percent? For instance, you do believe in studying World History but don't value, e.g., the lineage of all the British kings, which your department wants you to include in the course and which will be on a Departmental Final (some college departments do, in fact, do that.)

OK, most of what you have to teach you generally feel congruent. Then, when you come to the lineage of British kings, you can say to them, "Class, this stuff you may not find so exciting or valuable. Maybe you will. I hope so. But we've got to learn it. It's required on the Departmental Exam. So, stay with me, OK?" If you have been congruent all along, this honest congruent statement can often keep them with you as you bank on your previous authenticity with them.

You must understand that every minute of every class, every day, students may always be in a way asking: "Why the hell should we learn this stuff?" Sometimes they even ask it out loud. We are obligated to give them an authentic answer. They have a right to feel that this stuff matters. I myself am a bad math teacher mainly because I just don't "dig" math.

In summary, you need to work on being congruent with regard to: (1) your general interaction with your students; (2) your rules/procedures; (3) your delivery of your subject matter. It's work, but it is worth it. You'll have more rapport with your class. You'll have more credibility and influence with them, and less cause for disruptive behavior.

To practice these skills of *being congruent*, see chapter 9, "Training Exercises and Checklist."

NOTE

1. Carl Rogers, *On Encounter Groups* (New York: Harper and Row, 1970), 118.

Chapter Five

Using the Course Syllabus

A. USING THE COURSE SYLLABUS AS A "CONTRACT"

Many disruptive behaviors in college classrooms can not only be handled but *prevented* by having an effective, clear Course Syllabus. Your Course Syllabus should be given out as the first order of business at the first meeting of the class. As with the college catalogue, this Course Syllabus should be a "contract" with your students. It should specify how students will be graded, what you will generally cover in the course, and the standards you will enforce in general in your course, including some behavioral standards.

The Course Syllabus has weight because the students in your course are paying (or their families are paying) for their college education. And, since this is not compulsory education as it was in K–12, your students signed up for this course. Their time is valuable; they may have a job or family obligations. Thus, passing your course and heeding your requirements in your Course Syllabus gives you power to prevent disruptive behavior, if it is designed and thought out well.

You can decide how extensive you want it to be. You should design one that is congruent with your teaching style, your rules, procedures, and your department's requirements. It should even contain some behavioral norms that you want to be heeded during your course. You should explain each item in your

Course Syllabus carefully and ask if there are any questions for each item. If there are any arguments about your course policies, e.g., grading, you should be able to refer them to this clear Course Syllabus "contract." Therefore, it is essential that you clearly state your limits and standards well here.

B. WHAT IT SHOULD CONTAIN

If you want to be sure to curtail disruptive behaviors before they start, it would be best to include at least the following items in your Course Syllabus, designed congruently with how you really feel about these:

1. The course's catalogue number.
2. The name of the course.
3. Your name as instructor.
4. Your office hours.
5. The meeting times of the course.
6. How many credits are earned in this course.
7. A clear statement of your rules regarding certain behaviors.
8. A policy regarding cell phones, iPods, etc.
9. Your grading policy regarding quizzes, tests, Exams, field work, homework.
10. How class participation counts in the course.
11. Standards and due dates.
12. The correct format for the Final Papers.
13. The competencies or "exit requirements" for completing the course.
14. A tentative schedule of the topics that will be covered.
15. The required and supplemental reading assignments.
16. A tentative schedule of these reading assignments.
17. A tentative schedule of tests, Midterm, and Final Exam.
18. Your policies regarding: absence, lateness, leaving class early.
19. Your policy and consequences regarding cheating.
20. Your policy and consequences regarding plagiarism.
21. Your policy regarding students who need to bring their children to class.
22. Your policy regarding eating in class.

C. EXAMPLES OF DETAILED COURSE SYLLABI

Below are two examples of Course Syllabi. You can use these examples to design your own Course Syllabus. Of course, make sure that you design one that feels congruent for you.

Course Syllabus, Example 1

The first Course Syllabus is mine, one that I used the last time I taught this course. If you see an (*) next to the item, that means that when I gave this Syllabus out, I stopped at that item and explained it more orally. Notes for these oral explanations appear in the following section, D., "Clarifications for Course Syllabi."

ESC 301: Psychological Foundations of Secondary Education Spring 2008

Meets: Mon., Wed., Thurs. 12–2pm   4 credits

Prof. Howard Seeman Carmen Hall, Room 24 Phone: 960-8007

Email: *Hokaja@aol.com**

Office hours*: Mon. 11:30–12, 2–3; Wed. 11:30–12; 2–3; Th. 11:30–12; 2–3 or by Appointment.

I. The Exit Competencies to Pass this Course and Course Topics:

The student is able to:	*Tentative Calendar*
1. Explain the affective, ethical and cognitive requirements of being a quality teacher.	Jan. 30
2. Explain Carl Rogers on "the helping relationship"	Feb. 3
3. Explain Piaget's Stages of Cognitive Development	Feb. 5
4. Explain Erikson's Stages of Socio-Emotional Development	Feb. 10
5. Explain Maslow's Hierarchy of Needs Theory	Feb. 15
	Feb. 18 to 25 Spring Recess
6. Design a lesson plan for group instruction	March 2
7. Give an oral presentation on his/her major subject matter	March 3–20
8. Criticize problems in the major standardized tests	March 23
9. List the cues to look for in detecting child abuse (Midterm)	March 30
10. Design these kinds of tests: a) multiple choice; b) true/false; c) essay	April 3–10
11. Know the major sources of "classroom discipline problems"	April 13–15
12. Know methods for engaging students in classroom discussion	April 18–24
13. Design effective rules for the classroom, grades 9–10	April 27–30
14. Design effective rules for the classroom, grades 10–12	May 2–8

The student is able to:	*Tentative Calendar*
15. Design the classroom environment	May 11–15
16. Know the Pros and Cons of various seating arrangements	May 17–19
17. Final Exam	May 20
18. Term Paper (See Format Requirements below*) due	May 22

II. Requirements:

1. Attendance (3 absences = lower grade by ½, e.g., from B+ to B.)*
2. Punctuality (2 lates = 1 absence). The reason for the absence/lateness is not relevant. Students who miss fewer classes or are on time deserve more credit.*
3. Class participation required. Low class participation drops grade by ½; high class participation raises grade by ½ grade.*
4. Design one lesson plan for group instruction, due March 12: 10% of grade.
5. Give an oral presentation (date to be assigned): 10% of grade.
6. Hand in two designed tests (see 10 above) due: April 10; April 17; each 5% of grade.
7. Midterm (March 30) on the readings, lectures and discussions: 15% of grade.
8. Final Exam (May 20) on the readings, lectures and discussions: 35% of grade.
9. Paper (May 22) that discusses your abilities and watchful pitfalls for you as a teacher: 25% of grade.

(See section E. below: Formatting Requirements.)

III. *Tentative Reading Schedule:* TEXTS: E= Elliot's *Educational Psychology*

S= Seeman's *Preventing Discipline Problems*

Week of:	*Chapters:*
Feb. 12	E-3, 14
Feb. 19	S-6A
Feb. 26	E-6
March 4	E-7
March 11	E-10
March 18	E-12
March 25	E-15, 16 (not on Midterm)
April 10	E-5
April 17	E-4
April 24	S-4, 12
April 29	S-7, 10
May 6	S-8,11
May 12	S-9,13
May 15	E-17

IV. Classroom Behavior:

1. Students are expected to be attentive to the lectures/discussions in class, be on time, and not behave in any way that interferes with the learning of the other students or my teaching.
2. A student who is absent from class when a homework assignment was given, is still responsible for the homework when s/he returns to class. (Get the phone number or email address of one of your classmates.) Two late homework assignments are accepted with no penalty. After that, each late homework receives only ½ credit. Students who have not done the homework will not be called on to get class participation credit during the discussion of that homework.
3. If you come in late, do not talk to me at that time. Just take the empty seat by the door. I will only discuss lateness after class of at my office hours, however, I will explain further about lateness and absences.*
4. If you must leave the class early, take a seat near the door or in the back of the room so that you leave with the least disturbance. You are still responsible for all work.
5. If you need to bring a young child to class, you must ask my permission to do so; if the child disturbs the class, you will have to leave with the child.
6. If I suspect that you have cheated on a test, I will *not* tell you during the test. You will, instead, see that you have lost an additional 30 pts. on that test when you get it back. If you wish to discuss this, you will have to see me at my Office Hours right after class, not days later. At that time, if you contest the "cheating," I will give you an oral test on the same material. If you fail the oral test, then you lose one full grade on the final grade and it will be noted in your record. Or, you can just accept the situation, and do better on the next test. It is best "to not even look like you are cheating."*
7. I have many sophisticated, up-to-date methods for detecting plagiarism. I will uphold the college's policies here and will implement these consequences if you plagiarize. Thus, make sure that you give credit to any document that is not yours.
8. I prefer: no eating in class. However, if you must, make sure that it in no way disturbs my teaching or distracts the rest of the class.
9. Any hats/clothing that distracts other students' learning is not permitted in class.
10. Please turn off your cell phones in class; they are not to be used during class, e.g., no text messaging.

D. CLARIFICATIONS FOR COURSE SYLLABI

During my in-class review of the above Syllabus, I would stop at a few key sections to provide further details. Those sections, marked with (*) in the sample, are explained here.

1. As was mentioned above, this Course Syllabus should be explained to the class orally with a supportive, though firm tone when you go over it with them at the first meeting of the class.
2. Optional about including your email address. If you do include it, spell out the limits of its use, e.g., know when and how to refer students to other campus resources, establish clear policies about how soon and frequently you will respond to their emails.[1]
3. For your and your students' convenience, it is best to have Office Hours both before and after your class, e.g., to better handle and defer what might have been miscalls, handle needs for individual help instead of at class time.
4. Your Course Syllabus should be clear enough and well thought out enough that it not have ambiguities that can invite challenges.
5. Regarding lateness/absence:
   a. Here is *my* philosophy on this; you must find your own stance on this that is congruent for you. I tell my students something like this:
      "I cannot and will not investigate every reason for your lateness/ absence. Out in the world, at a job, if you are sick and late or absent a lot, the boss might send you a "get well" card. But he might still have to get another employee to replace you! If you do not do well in this course because of extenuating circumstances, you still have not done well in the course. My job is to uphold standards and give more credit to those who are here to participate in the class. If I do not do this, the degree you are working for will lose value. If you are absent or late too much, perhaps you should take this course at another time, drop it, rather than fail it."
      (Using this policy above usually impedes the creation of students' clever alibis.)
   b. You may also want to use this method: Students are marked absent once they have come in late, when you have already taken attendance. If they want their "absence" fixed to a "late," they must see you after class, not during the class. If they forget, they are/were marked absent. And, for example, three absences = losing five points on their Final Grade.
   c. Another method: if you do not want to call the roll at every class, you can pass around an attendance sheet that they must all sign at the first meeting of the class, or at an early meeting of the class after late registration is done. Then, to guard against forgeries, make many copies of this signed sheet, enough for the whole semester, with blank spaces where they can sign in next to their original signature, where you can see that it is authentically their signature. (You may want to warn them that a forgery will, for example, go on to their record.)

    d. If you are sure a "physical/health problem" is real (a doctor's note?) allow students flexibility in your Course Syllabus' requirements— however, make sure that this flexible policy is clearly spelled out.

6. Regarding homework excuses, you may want to adopt this attitude:

"If your homework is late because, e.g., your dog ate your homework once, or twice, you're still OK. However, three late homework loses ten points. By the third time, you need to get another dog."

Revise this to fit what is congruent for you. Also, do not fall into generally accepting late homeworks. If you do, you will have fewer and fewer students doing the homework on time, as each sees that they can hand the homework in late. Then, you will have less quality class participation— since only fewer and fewer will have done the homework on time for a quality class discussion.

7. Plagiarism: Again, this is not best handled by disciplining a student in front of the class. It is best handled by giving back his/her paper with no grade at the top, but instead with: "See me at my office hours." Then, you should carry out your department/college's policy here. (See Policy on Plagiarism in Course Syllabus Example 2.)

8. Regarding class participation, you may wish to convey something like the following: "I feel that shyness, when you're three years old, may be cute. But, when you get older and in college, it's a disability! Shy people get fewer dates, have fewer friends, and are hired and promoted less. Of course, I will be supportive of anyone who has difficulty speaking in class. Please write to me if you feel that; I want to help. (Don't worry about spelling.) Or see me at an office hour, and I will try to help you. But, those who participate in class do deserve more credit."

You may want to say some version of this: "If English is your second language, I admire you. I think English is a very difficult language, and I am less capable than you here: I can only speak one language. However, please make sure if you need help here, it is done without disrupting other students during the class. Meanwhile, please risk speaking in class. I will be very supportive of your courage to speak a second language. Again, I cannot, and would also be nervous speaking another language in a class of mostly native speakers. So, I admire you."

Course Syllabus, Example 2

AS 3112
The American People
Fall, 2008
Professors: R. B. and E. E.

Phone: (000) 000-0000
Office: B220, 221
Office Hours: Tuesday and Thursday, 12:30- 2:30 PM, or by Appointment
Email: R. B. —@aol.com; E. E. —@aol.com

Required Books

Eric Foner, *Give Me Liberty, An American History*, Volume 1
R. D. Heffner (ed.), A *Documentary History of the United States*
Thomas Paine, *Common Sense;* Benjamin Franklin, *Autobiography*
Henry Louis Gates (ed.), *Classic Slave Narratives*
Horatio Alger, *Ragged Dick*

Course Description

From a chronological viewpoint, API is the first part of the API & II. You can take them in any sequence. This course explores some of the major social and political currents in US history, from the earliest contact of Africans and Europeans with the Americas in the 15th and 16th centuries, to the end of the of Civil War. Course topics include: cultural contact and exchange; the origins of the colonies; early systems of labor such as indentured servitude and slavery; The Declaration of Independence, the American Revolution, and the Constitution.

The course is a part of the General Education Program and can be counted for G.E. credit in the U.S. History cluster. The American People can be taken in any sequence.

Goals and Objectives

- Students will demonstrate an overall understanding of the changing conditions in the US in the period under study.
- Students will have some idea of the major events and figures of the period.
- Students will understand the racial and class tensions that informed the period.
- Students will demonstrate an analysis of some more specialized aspect of the period through individual analytical papers.
- Students will demonstrate an ability to analyze a historical document.

Course Requirements

- A midterm and final.
- Attendance will be taken and you will be required to attend all classes. Three unexcused absences will mean a reduction of ½ a letter grade. If you come in after attendance is called, you will receive half a credit for attendance.
- Two long papers.
- Readings should be done on the date required. You will be required to summarize, that is, list the 5 main points about readings indicated in the Syllabus.

We will collect and grade these readings. If your list is: "inadequate," such will be noted. Three "inadequates" on these readings = a reduction of ½ a letter grade on your final grade.
- One low grade will be dropped if you have done all of the assignments. These assignments should be typed.
- If you plagiarize from a book, net or another student you will get an F.
- Your participation is expected and your grade will depend partly on that participation: At the end of each week, I will note who has participated in the class: good questions, besides comments/opinions. At the end of the semester, if you have participated much less than most in the class, your grade will drop by ½ a letter grade. If you have participated more than most in the class, your grade will be raised by ½ a letter grade. Reminder: "shyness" is a disability. (I will explain in section D 8.)

Syllabus (Part I)

Aug 26:	Syllabus handed out. Go to Bookstore and Buy Books
Aug 28:	Introduction to Course Read: in Foner, Chapter 1 pp. 1–35
Sept 2 and 4:	Lecture: Colonial Background Read: Foner, Chapter 2 pp. 36–70
Sept 9:	Lecture: The American Revolution and Republican Ideology Read: "The Declaration Of Independence," in *Documents*
Sept 16:	Discussion of *Common Sense* Read: Finish *Common Sense.* bring book to class Hand in the summary of the 5 major points in *Common Sense.*
Sept 18:	Debate on pros and cons of the American Revolution. Begin *The Autobiography of Benjamin Franklin.* Bring *Common Sense* to class
Sept 23:	The Constitution and the Consolidation of the Revolution "Federalist, Number 10" in *Documents* & Read: Foner, pp. 211–240.
Sept 25:	Class Discussion of "Federalist No. 10" Read: Finish and No.10 Holiday Rosh Hashanah, Read: *Autobiography of Benjamin Franklin*
Oct 2:	Class Discussion: Franklin Read: Finish Franklin; bring book to class
Oct 7:	Conflicts in the New Nation, Jefferson/Hamilton, Foner pp. 241–271 Holiday Yom Kippur, Work on Assignment Written Assignment: Due October 16, 4 to 6 *typed* pages. Choose 1 or 2: In order to do this assignment, you need to read Paine, Federalist #10 and Franklin carefully and attend class lectures and debates. You need to use the texts and class notes in order to make an argument.

1. Pretend you are a living in the British colony of North America on the eve of the revolution. How did Paine's ideas of democracy and independence affect you? How did the work ethic of Franklin's help you to understand new American ideals and the new values of leadership, work, independence, and discipline? How did both Paine's and Franklin's ideas make you an activist in the revolution? Or did these new ideals threaten your loyalty to England? Why?
2. Compare and contrast Paine's idea of government: direct, simple democracy, the majority and its role with the views expressed in James Madison's " Federalist No. 10." How are they different, how are they the same?

Oct 14:   The Growth of the Southern Slavery
            Read- begin "Frederick Douglass in *Classic Slave Narratives* and Foner pp. 110–124 and Chapter 11, pp. 337–365.
Oct 16:   King Cotton, Continue "Frederick Douglass" Read Zinn, Chapter 9

            Assignment Due, points will be taken off for late papers
Oct 21:   Midterm Exam Review
Oct 23:   Midterm Exam
            Make up given only on Oct 28 and will be much harder

Accommodations for Students with Special Needs

If you have or suspect you may have a physical, psychological, medical or learning disability that may impact your course work, please contact the Office for Students with Disabilities (OSSD). Phone: 516-876-3005. Fax: 516-876-3083, TTD: 516-876-3083, LupardoW@oldwestbury.edu. The office will help you determine if you qualify for accommodations and help you get them. All support services are free and all contacts with the OSSD are strictly confidential.

*Policy on Plagiarism

Plagiarism and cheating are condemned at all institutions of higher learning. These acts detract from the student's intellectual and personal growth by undermining the processes of studying, reading, note-taking and struggling with one's own expression of ideas and information. Moreover, cheating inevitably involves secrecy and exploitation of others. See "Academic Integrity" and related topics in the *Old Westbury Catalog, 2006–2008*, p.46. Plagiarizing means "presenting somebody else's words or ideas without acknowledging where those words and ideas come from" (Ann Raimes, *Keys for Writers*, fifth ed., p. 188). Examples include: copying material from the Internet or other sources and presenting it as your own; using any author's words without quotation marks;

using any quotation without credit; changing any author's words slightly and presenting them as your own; using ideas from any published sources (even in your own words) without exact credit. (This includes all material from the Internet or electronic databases.)

Also includes: using long passages in a paper that have been written or rewritten by a friend or tutor; turning in any assignment written by someone else.

However, using quotations or borrowed ideas while giving exact credit is good academic procedure. Other types of academic dishonesty include unauthorized collaboration or copying of students' work (cheating); falsifying grades or evaluations; and others. They are treated as equivalent to plagiarism. When detected and verified, plagiarism and other academic dishonesty will be punished severely. Normally, the first offense will result in a failure on the specific assignment; a second offense or a particularly flagrant first offense will result in failing the course. Know what plagiarism is and how to avoid it; for guidance see Raimes or any other college writing handbook. *Please note: in this matter, ignorance is never an acceptable excuse.*

I hope that these two examples of Course Syllabi above were helpful to you as you design/revise your own Course Syllabus that is congruent with *your* style. Also, keep in mind while you design your own Course Syllabus that most of your responses to disruptive behaviors are best handled with: "See me after class" or at your office hours. If your Course Syllabus "contract" is clear and detailed enough, it will prevent and handle most miscalled behaviors.

For the most part, your students are: motivated to pass your course, to attain a satisfactory grade, to complete course requirements, to obtain a college degree, to earn status, to get a better job, to make more money, are paying (or their families are) for this course, and/or will lose any student financial aid if their grades are too low. So, these motivations and a clear Course Syllabus will often handle/prevent many disruptive behaviors. Most College Freshmen Orientation classes will prepare students for these course norms in Course Syllabi even before they have entered your class. Or, you can recommend that Freshmen Orientation classes include these issues in *their* Course Syllabi.

E. GUIDELINES FOR STUDENT TERM PAPERS

Though not disruptive to your classroom teaching, many college professors struggle with the hassle of poorly handed in, poorly formatted Term Papers.

The best way to assure quality Term Papers is to have students work on these papers in steps, rather than just handing them in completed, in one fell swoop, when done.

Instead:

a. They can first confer with you about the viability of their topic;
b. They can bring you the list of books they will consult and research for the paper, to head them off from just copying from the Internet;
c. They can submit a detailed outline of the paper for your feedback.

Then, you can also state the Format Requirements for the Term Paper in your Course Syllabus. Such can save you a lot of work and student arguments. These below are only my recommendations. Of course, revise these to fit your own congruence:

1. I will read only your first few paragraphs of your Term Paper for grammar, spelling problems. If you have too many errors in these first few paragraphs, the same problems usually persist throughout the paper. If this is the case, I will not read it any further, but hand your paper back to you for you to work on these corrections. Then, you can re-submit it.
2. If you hand the paper in again with these problems, you will need to go to the Writing Lab for writing help. Then, in order for me to accept your paper again, you must bring me a note from the Writing Lab (or a tutor) that you did attend at least one remedial session. If the problem persists, you may receive an INC. for the course until I can verify that your writing has become satisfactory.
3. Do not hand in papers with fancy bindings.
4. Do not "dog-ear" your papers. They should be stapled in the corner, or held together by the binder. Also, careful: paper clips tend to fall off; I do not recommend these.
5. All papers should be double-spaced, in Font: *Times Roman*, font size 12.
6. If I specify a minimum length of the paper, understand that huge margins and spaces at the top or bottom does not make the paper *longer*.
    Make sure that:
    • You number all the pages.
    • There is a Title Page in the front of your paper with:
    • Your full name as it appears on your registration for this course.
    • Your college student I.D. no.
    • The title of your paper.
    • The title of this course.
    • My name as your instructor.
    • The date you handed it in.
7. Always save your paper on your computer as you write (hit *save* often) and make sure that you keep an extra copy of your paper.

I hope the above possible stipulations for the Term Paper were helpful to you designing your own. Regarding this whole chapter, again, if you can follow the suggestions above, you will prevent, not just handle, disruptive behaviors in your college classes.

For practice making an effective Course Syllabus, see chapter 9, "Training Exercises and Checklist."

NOTE

1. Tomorrow's Professor at http://amps-tools.mit.edu/tomprofblog/archives/2007/11/828_setting_bou.html.

Chapter Six

Engaging Teaching Methods

A. Teaching Methods: Pitfalls
B. Repairing Pitfalls: 35 Engagement Methods

A. TEACHING METHODS: PITFALLS

It's simple: if the students turn off and tune out, they are more apt to act out. If they are engaged in your teaching, following the train of what you are teaching, they are less apt to get off that train and cause problems. Thus, you need to use teaching methods whereby students act into the learning, instead of acting out. An *in*effective delivery style of teaching fuels disruptive behavior.

Unfortunately, most teachers tend to teach the way they were taught. And most teachers were taught by teachers entrenched in a philosophy of education that is not conducive enough to learning, to learning that is intrinsically interesting and that enriches students' lives. Instead, the traditional educational philosophy teaches too much rote learning, and too often is just cognitive and not affective enough. We have tended to teach too much for just explaining, predicting, and controlling things. Yet, to be successful in our lives, we need emotional learning and emotional awareness, social skills, empathy training, experiential-affective knowledge, not just cognitive understandings and calculations. Our society is not suffering from a lack of its ability to explain, predict, and control, but from issues such as divorce, alcoholism, drug abuse, loneliness, thrill seeking to counter boredom, lack of emotional understandings, and low self-esteem that leads to violence.

Thus, the traditional educational philosophy has wrongly emphasized: standardized tests, top-down curricula, memorizing facts, rewards and punishments to motivate compliance,[1] and too much passive-listener lecturing to/at students, especially in colleges.

We must try to steer against this entrenched tradition, one of the main causes of college disruptive behavior on the rise. As these disruptive behaviors enter our colleges, we should not just apply more compliance; this is not high school, nor should it be this way throughout K–12. Instead, we need to revise our teaching methods so that we motivate students to act into the learning, so that we do not need to force compliance.

The traditional teaching style, which has these pitfalls below, fuels disruptive behavior:

A. You only lecture; you do not involve the students in your teaching.
B. Your teaching pace slows down, perhaps due to your handling too many student distractions/questions, such that students start to leave "the train of your lesson."
C. The class cannot feel that the instructor is congruent with what you are teaching. Your teaching seems to come from a "tape" in your head rather than from your "heart." The students do not feel that you really care about what you are teaching.
D. There is too little emotional, affective content in your teaching; it is just too cognitive.
E. The way that you are teaching is too abstract; there are too few experiences and examples to really make the learning concrete for the students.
F. Your teaching seldom relates to the students' experiences. It is hard for them to feel the relevance of what you are teaching.
G. The material to be learned is being fed to the students only by you. There is little chance during your class for the students to interact with each other, to enliven and digest these learnings with each other; they are inactive learners.
H. The students cannot feel a sense of order in what you are teaching; they are not sure where you are going with this point, or where the train of your teaching is going. There is little felt sense of order in what you are teaching from *their* point of view, though *you* know where you are going.
I. They do not understand some of what you are teaching and you provide few ways for them to let you know this during your teaching—until it is too late, when they show you this by doing poorly on your test.

B. REPAIRING PITFALLS: 35 ENGAGEMENT METHODS

If you can mend these pitfalls (A–I), students will be less likely to "turn off," "tune out," and then "act out" in your class. Here are some teaching methods that you may use to mend each of the above pitfalls.

A. You only lecture; you do not involve the students in your teaching.

1. *Use the Interactive Methods Suggested Below.* Try not to be just the "sage on the stage."

B. Your teaching pace slows down, perhaps due to your handling too many student distractions/questions, such that students start to leave "the train of your lesson."

2. *Remind Them of the Schedule.* Now that you have told the class of the Topic Schedule, Reading Schedule, Test and Final Exam Schedule in your Course Syllabus, you can make use of these to prevent disruptive behaviors. At any given time during your teaching, if you find that student disruptions are becoming too frequent, you can say something like the following to your class:

   "Class, notice on the Course Syllabus that we are supposed to be here by this date, but we are falling behind. You will have a Midterm on March 20 that will cover these topics and readings. I am hoping to spend a lot of class time helping you understand all of these. But, if my teaching is disrupted too often, I will have to stop to police these problems. That is a waste of my time, the knowledge and skills I want to give you, and a waste of your time and money. However, whether I cover these fully in class or not, you still will be responsible for these on the Midterm. Please. Try to help me help you. Thank you." (Of course, revise this statement to fit your congruent style.)

   The above will not only talk directly to the disruptive students without naming them, but will also put peer pressure on these disruptive students to not impede the class's learning.

C. The class cannot feel that the instructor is congruent with what you are teaching. Your teaching seems to come from a "tape" in your head rather than from your "heart." The students do not feel that you really care about what you are teaching.

3. *Make a Congruent Preface Statement.* Before you launch into the content of the curriculum, level with the students and tell them how you honestly feel about teaching them what you are about to teach. Or, tell them how you honestly feel about the importance or value of the content you are about to teach.

4. *Talk More in the First Person.* Use "I" a lot. Even if the topic is applicable to many people, or all, or "we," use "I." If it is applicable to many or all,

use yourself as an example as often as you can. This will make you more of a congruent *teacherperson* to your students, instead of just *The Teacher*, which will give less fuel for them to want to revolt against authority.

D. There is too little emotional, affective content in your teaching; it is just too cognitive.

5. *Try to Follow Some Student Digressions.* Though you may have to watch out for digressions that take you too far from the subject, sometimes these digressions are student motivational feelings that can support what you are teaching. Let students share their feelings and personal experiences that are kicked off by the material that you are teaching. However, be diligent in channeling these feelings and experiences into transferable knowledge. There's no harm in noting on the chalkboard their feelings (and ideas) besides yours, and then relating both later.

6. *"How Do You Feel about This Topic?"*. Simply stop from time to time during your teaching and ask: "How do you feel about this topic?" "Which seems more meaningful to you, valuable?" "Why?"

7. *Ask Them to List:* the valuable information learned in this topic. Now, ask them to prioritize these from most valuable to least by giving each one a number, e.g., 1–4. Then, they might share their prioritized list and explain their feelings for their priorities. Again, acceptance and sharing of these feelings is the goal here, not right or wrong answers, at least at this point.

E. The way that you are teaching is too abstract; there are too few experiences and examples to really make the learning concrete for the students.

8. *Have Students Role-Play:* famous people in history, characters in literature, or famous people in science. Also, have them personify concepts, even parts of speech, e.g., be a verb, a gerund. What would a gerund say, dress like, do? Personify any abstraction: infinity, chemical elements, the earth, the sun, the "woods" in Frost's "Stopping by the Woods," democracy, a law, Congress, France, the Alps, the Pythagorean Theorem, etc. Students might role-play a person or topic while the class guesses who they are.

   Role-playing is a skill. You can't just tell students to be, for example, George Washington. This skill takes training and practice.

   Some tips here will be helpful:

   a. Do a warm up; discuss the topic and relax the class; let them discuss it intellectually first.

b. Look for a student who seems most open, "most ready," who is somewhat extroverted.

c. Ask this person to picture, e.g., George Washington.

d. Ask this student some questions that define the role, e.g., "What would he be wearing?" "How would he sit?"

e. Ask the student to show you what he means, e.g., "You mean he'd sit like 'this'?" "No?" "Then, how?" "Show me."

f. Now, talk to the student (supportively) as if he is George Washington.

9. *The Empty Chair Technique.* Place an empty chair in front of the room. Ask students to imagine, e.g., a historical figure in the chair, or a character from a work of literature, or a famous scientist sitting in the chair. Ask volunteers to come and sit in the empty chair. Have the class say hello to this person and ask, "Hi, who are you?" Let the one in the chair now answer. Have the class talk to him or her, ask a question, and so on. You can take notes on this imaginative discussion, and later use your notes for a full class discussion after the exercise is over. Let the interview go on without you interrupting to make corrections. You can do that later. (Here again, the guidelines I gave above for role-playing can also be helpful.)

F. Your teaching seldom relates to the students' experiences. It is hard to feel the relevance of what you are teaching.

10. *Teach Using a Confluent Lesson Approach.* A "confluent lesson" is an inductive lesson that teaches affective and cognitive learning simultaneously. The teacher should proceed as follows:

a. Choose a real concern that your students have. Some concerns might be: dealing with conflicts, future worries, being understood, being bored, money problems, arguments with their parents, or not having a good weekend.

b. Invite your students to share these concerns in a structured way. For instance, ask them to list their conflicts and angers, future worries, areas they feel misunderstood, what they find boring.

c. Ask them to either prioritize these, correlate them, or notice similarities among them. For instance, "Which conflicts have to do with power, money, rules, lifestyles?" Or "What kinds of future worries do you notice, any categories?" Or "How do these misunderstandings happen?" Or "What makes some things meaningful, others meaningless?"

d. The class might analyze all of these by listing them on the chalkboard. Here, the whole class might inductively find similarities, differences, correlations, and causes between the items. The teacher then can ask them to draw arrows relating items 1 and 6, or 7 and 2, . . . and ask them why they see a relationship here.

e. Finally, the class is asked to make generalizations from noticing the relations they do find among their own shared experiences. Regarding their conflicts, they may be led by you to discover that many conflicts they presently experience can also be found in, e.g., actual historic wars. You might then assign them to "Write down three things about the causes of the, e.g., Civil War that are similar to conflicts we listed on the chalkboard today." Or, you might assign them to "Choose three characters in, e.g., *Tale of Two Cities* who have worries and angers similar to those we named on the chalkboard here."

f. Of course, each class will discuss different learnings. And although you must now follow them and take notes (besides them), they are now concerned about what you are teaching because the lesson was built on and out of their own concerns.

11. *Future Projection.* Ask the students to write a letter imagining it is five years or ten years later. Ask them to write out where they are living now, what they are doing with their time. Are they married? Have children? They write the letter dated, e.g., May 6, 2014 and write it in the present tense. If you're teaching an English class, the class shares these compositions in a non-judgmental way, and only later do you evaluate them for grammar. If it's a literature class, you might assign a poem or short story that also struggles with future projection: e.g., Frost's "Stopping by the Woods," Wilder's *Our Town*, Orwell's *1984*. Then, you'll need to assign "theme questions" that relate their own future projections to the work of literature. If you're teaching History, you might ask that the future projection be about political matters: Who's president? Are countries at war? Why? You might then assign them readings that explore these predictions. Or they might have to find facts that make these predictions plausible.

G. The material to be learned is being fed to the students only by you. There is little chance during your class for the students to interact with each other, to enliven and digest these learnings with each other; they are inactive learners.

12. *Better Seating Arrangement.* Instead of always having the seats in rows, *try* working in a horseshoe or circle. Students can see each other and hear each other's comments and questions better. They also have the benefit of being able to see nonverbal reactions that often support their courage

to speak up. However, working in a highly participatory circle or horseshoe requires more skill on the part of the teacher.

Here are some helpful suggestions for working in a horseshoe/circle seating arrangement:

a. Get into the habit of standing up and giving very short lectures on the curriculum topic (no longer than five minutes).

b. Then, direct the class to react to what you just said, and sit down and don't talk; let the class talk, share, and react. Stay out of this discussion.

c. You can have the students call on each other, rather than you; the last person to speak calls on someone who raises their hand after the current speaker is done, and so on.

d. However, you might call on people, disentangle mis-listenings, and just be a "gatekeeper" of the flow of the discussion.

e. When you think the discussion has served its purpose of reacting to your little lecture, stand up again, and summarize the class reactions.

f. Then, deliver another short lecture, and sit down and repeat the above procedures. Also, no one interrupts you when you're standing, and you don't interrupt them when you sit down. Enforce this routine. In this way you can channel the participatory energy of the circle or horseshoe arrangement.

g. If your class is too large to work in a circle or horseshoe, have the class form concentric circles, where a smaller circle is inside the larger one. The inner circle participates for a while, then the students switch seats. Now the students who were in the inner circle—observe the new inner circle participants.

13. *Delay Calling on Students.* Tell the students that you will not call on the first people to raise their hands because you are giving the whole class time to think. Validate the slower thinkers by reminding the class (and yourself) that the fastest answer is rarely well thought out and is certainly not always right. Real thought takes effort. If you expect thoughtful answers from your students, you have to give them the time to formulate them.

14. *Be Aware of Poor Questioning Techniques.* Asking the class questions does get them to participate. However, often teachers ask poor questions or fall into certain pitfalls that curtail the participation that good questioning can encourage. Be aware of these poor questioning mistakes:

a. Don't ask a "complex question," e.g., "Who knows a cause of the Civil War and how the South reacted to it?" Instead, ask one question as simply as you can at a time.

b. Don't ask "railroading" questions that push the answer you want, e.g., "Who knows a cause of the Civil War, that was an economic one, that had to do with Southern agriculture?"

    c. Avoid questions that require simply memory answers, e.g., "Who was president during the Civil War?" "What was the final battle of the Civil War?" or "What do you call the 'ing' form of a verb?" Such questions do not encourage class participation. The class's involvement is over as soon as someone has the remembered answer.

    d. Avoid questions that can be answered by simply "Yes" or "No," e.g., "Did the South win the Civil War?"

    e. Don't call on the first person who raises his/her hand. Instead, wait until a few hands are up before you call on someone. This will discourage the competitive race to the correct answer and give students a chance to think and get courage to raise their hands.

    f. Don't always respond "correct" to the first student's answer. Allow a few answers to be tried before you let them know who is correct. This will encourage them to listen to each other more, and keep thinking.

15. *Encouragement/Repetition.*

    a. Ask them to raise their hands high and look around the room when they raise their hands. Then, they will see that they are not alone with their answer or question, which will encourage more students to risk their answer or question.

    b. Don't repeat every comment, answer, or question each student gives or asks so the other students can hear them. Don't become a P.A. system for the class. If you repeat their responses for the rest of the class, you encourage them not to listen to each other and only listen to you. Instead, say, "good" to John's answer, and leave it at that. If students didn't hear John's answer, ask them to ask John, and John talks to the class, not you.

16. *Note Student Responses on the Chalkboard.* Don't just use the chalkboard for your notes. Also, record their ideas on the chalkboard, perhaps in response to a question you put to them. And don't revise their responses into the "correct way" to say it. That'll turn them off. Keep it in their language. Write their responses by listing them by letter: A, B, C, not 1, 2, 3. Then, after all responses are on the chalkboard, ask the class to prioritize them. Should "A" be 3 or 1 or 2? Should "C" be 1? Ask them to number the lettered items in order of most important or most valuable or most difficult. Then discuss their opinions of their ordering of these lettered items. Or ask them to "U" the item they most understand or agree with, "X" items they don't understand, or disagree with, and "?" items they have questions about. Then, discuss their markings per item.

17. *Have Them Teach Each Other.* From the above method, you might ask those who made a checkmark on an item, e.g., B, to talk to those who made an "U." Or ask all of those who marked a "?" to raise their hands.

Now have a student who marked a "U" for this item teach the one who has the "?" question.

18. *Use 3×5 Cards.* To encourage free responses, you might ask the class a question and have them all respond on 3×5 cards that you hand out. The students write their question or answer on the 3×5 card anonymously. You then collect them face down and shuffle them. You can then read them all, or read some, or pass them back out to the class who reads them to the class. The class might try to guess who wrote each comment or answer.

19. *Paired-Off Interviews.* Ask the class a question. Then, ask them to turn to their neighbor and interview each other about their answer to this question. Instruct them that when they finish the interview of their neighbor, they will have to summarize what their neighbor said. This will not only encourage more participation but force them to listen to each other.

20. *Let Them Be the Teacher.* After you have taught a segment of the topic, ask, "Who knows it well enough to teach it?" Get a volunteer and ask him/her to now "be the teacher." Ask the class to make believe they don't understand the segment just taught and to ask this "teacher" some questions. By having the opportunity to briefly be the teacher, students can be continually rewarded for their learning. And the students who make up questions, even fake ones, learn the topic even better by trying to do this.

21. *Collaboration.* Every so often allow the class for a brief time to *break off into small groups* to discuss something you've initiated. When they return to the large groups, have a representative of each small group present his/her group's findings. This procedure will encourage each group to listen to the other groups' comments.

22. *Panel Discussions and Debates.* Set up a panel of students to discuss an issue. Also, give the class a sheet of questions they should keep in mind as the panel discussion proceeds. Then, the whole class responds to the panel. If it's a debate, the class can argue from side to side, and vote.

23. *Have the Class Create Questions for the Class.* After you have taught a short unit, ask the class to create some good questions one might ask on this unit. Then, students ask each other questions. You should hold yourself back as long as you can if you hear wrong answers being given; the attention to each other may be more useful than your always taking over with the right answer. You can always make some corrections at the end of the period. Take notes if you must.

24. *Students Test the Class.* Have students, at their desks, each write two sentences, one that is true about the topic you taught yesterday, and one that is incorrect. Then, ask for volunteers to go up to the blackboard and each

volunteer write one true and one incorrect statement on the blackboard—
till the blackboard is filled with twenty or so statements, some correct
about the topic, some not. (You can use many colored chalks.) Then ask:
"OK, who can see a sure incorrect statement up there?" When they point
out one, do not say correct or incorrect. Let the class vote; if a large minority appears in this show of hands, let them debate the statement; you
stay out of it for a while.

25. *Increase the Trust Level of the Class.* You will have more class participation if the students feel safe responding and sharing their own ideas and
feelings. To do this you can be a model and share *your* feelings. Also, try
to protect other students' opinions and feelings. Do not allow disrespect
of another student's opinions. You can even demand that if you want to
disagree, you must first summarize what the last student said. This will
foster more empathetic listening.

H. The students cannot feel a sense of order in what you are teaching; they are not sure where you are going with this point, or where the train of your teaching is going. There is little felt sense of order in what you are teaching from *their* point of view, though *you* know where you are going.

26. *Write on the Chalkboard a "Felt" Goal. Not an "Aim" for the Lesson.*
Don't write on the chalkboard, e.g., "Aim: To learn about imperialism."
Since the class doesn't understand "imperialism," this will give them no
real feeling for where you are going. Instead of presenting an abstraction
as your "Aim," give them a "felt goal," some goal they can understand or
feel. For instance: "We will learn how and why people sometimes push
their ideas, feelings, and power on others." They can understand and feel
this goal. Here, you can start your teaching with an everyday example of
this e.g., "push of power on others," and then lead to an understanding of
"imperialism" as an international phenomenon. Similarly, in an English
class, an "Aim" such as "to study Orwell's *1984*" would not be as helpful
as the felt goal: "to discover how losing freedom feels." Similarly, in a
math class, an "Aim" such as "to study the Pythagorean theorem" would
not be as helpful as the felt goal: "to figure out the length of side A of
the triangle, when we only know sides B and C." A felt goal rather than
an abstract "Aim" gives the lesson a sense of felt order.

27. *Give an Overview When You Begin.* Besides presenting a "felt goal,"
also give a brief overview of where you intend to go. You might even
give your overview in an outline form. For instance, "Class, today we
will . . . (felt goal), then (A) we will . . . ,then (B) we'll try to . . . , (C)

finally we'll see . . . ." The overview will also give students a felt sense of order.

28. *Stop Every Once in A While and Review.* "What We've Covered, Where We Are, and Where We're Going": After you've covered some material, refer back to your "felt goal," point to where you are now (perhaps at a certain point on the chalkboard notes), and point to (or say) where you are going. Do this two or three times during your teaching. Also ask, "How many see where we are? Raise your hands." This procedure will keep the students on track with the train of what you are teaching.

29. *Summarize Often.* After you have taught a few segments of the subject matter, summarize what you have taught within a brief statement, then move on. Do this often. This will give your teaching momentum.

I. They do not understand some of what you are teaching and you provide few ways for them to let you know this during your teaching—until it is too late, when they show you this by doing poorly on your test.

30. *Check Understanding.* Before you move on to the next task or content to be taught, *ask a brief question that will give you feedback* as to whether they understand, or are ready or not to go on.

31. *Ask for Volunteers*, rather than pick on students who feel uncomfortable. Then, treat the volunteers very supportively. The shy ones will be watching as to whether it's safe to venture volunteering. If you treat the students who even give wrong answers well, you will get more volunteers. Provide safe ways for students to respond. Thank them, praise their responses, even if they are not correct.

32. *Total Responses.* Instead of asking, e.g., "Any questions?" say: "Raise your hand very high if you follow me; not so high if you follow me only somewhat; don't raise your hand if you feel a little lost. OK? Ready? Go. Now, look around the room. See? You're not alone." This procedure will show you more than the procedure of asking the ones with low confidence to do the most, viz., "raise their hand." Eventually, you only need to say: "How many follow me well, not so well?" Or "Got me?" Students will readily learn to raise their hands high or not at all to show you where they are. This will give you easy ongoing feedback about their learning. The traditional way—"Any questions?"—asks the non-confident students to show they are not confident in front of their peers: obviously an educationally unsound technique for them, and for you getting good feedback.

33. *Let Them Create the Questions.* Have all in row one create a question
    about what you just taught, a question that can even feign ignorance
    about the topic. Then, have row one turn to row two (to couple off) and
    row one asks row two their question. Row two teaches the answer. Row
    three asks, row four teaches, etc. Let them talk to each other doing this
    for about five minutes. Then, ask: "Any partners in this exercise now
    have a question?" You will then get some very good questions, since
    they first were able to do this privately. And, the "teachers" in the rows
    will have learned the topic better by having to explain and teach it to the
    other students.
34. *Use a Lot of Visuals.* Bring in maps, actual objects, use PowerPoint pre-
    sentations, diagram things often, show films, and when possible: go to
    the place you are talking about.
35. *Give Them Notes to Follow.* Often students are poor note takers. Some-
    times you can give them "notes" to follow, call them "starter notes,"
    where they have the "outline" of what you will teach, which guides their
    learning as they fill it in.

To work on using and designing Engagement Methods for your teaching,
the reader should see chapter 9, "Training Exercises and Checklist."

For fifty-seven more strategies for better student engagement, the reader is
referred to Prof. Howard Seeman's *Preventing Classroom Discipline Problems*, third edition (Lanham, MD: Rowman & Littlefield Education, 1999).

NOTE

1. This sentence was inspired by an article about President Obama's choosing of a
Secretary of Education that appeared in *The Nation*, Dec. 29, 2008 by Alfie Kohn.

Chapter Seven

Strengthening Your Assertiveness

A. Factors that Weaken Assertiveness
B. Working on Your Blocks to Assertiveness

Another way to *prevent* disruptive behavior is for the class to see that you follow through with what you say in class and in your Course Syllabus. Do not fool yourself: it is easy to just not bother to do what you said you would do. But, if you take this easy tack, if you do not follow through, your credibility will wane with your students, and they will slowly know that you do not really mean what you say or warn. Then, you will plant the seeds for behaviors that may become very bothersome, more bothersome than following through.

One problem here is that often teachers lack the strength to assert themselves to follow through. All the advice discussed in the past chapters will not be implemented well unless the instructor has the ability to assert him/herself. Some people can take stands, step up to the plate and assert themselves when the need arises, while others are torn, afraid and/or weak in this area.

If this is a problematic area for you, your students can usually tell. So, no matter how well you understand the previous chapters, you may be prone to have many class disruptions if you do not have the ability to assert yourself well. However, we can locate the causes that weaken and block your assertiveness and remedy these.

A. FACTORS THAT WEAKEN ASSERTIVENESS

1. *Guilt:* If you do not really care about the subject matter you are presenting, if you are incongruent, inauthentic, do what you like rather than what

is good for your students, do not hand back papers/tests timely, or are unfair—you will feel, even if you hide it well: guilty. Or you are guilty even outside your work as a teacher, e.g., you owe someone something, you lied, you haven't done your share of *x*, or you should've called your friend, etc. This guilt will weaken your sense of self-worth and also your ability to assert yourself.

2. *Conflicting Feelings:* You won't be able to say "No" well if you feel partly "Yes" and partly "No." You need to sort out your feelings where you feel ambivalent, especially regarding your rules, grades, standards and boundaries with your students. Perhaps you need to say "Maybe"; but then you need to get clear on the conditions for deciding. You will need to do this when you make up your Course Syllabus (see chapter 5). You can't uphold this "contract" and assert yourself if you are ambivalent.

3. *Fear of Others' Anger:* You won't be able to assert yourself if you are afraid of other people's anger or that they may "punish" you in some way for expressing this anger.

4. *Fear of Your Own Anger:* You won't be able to assert yourself well if you are afraid that you'll get so angry that you won't be able to control yourself.

5. *Low Ego:* If you feel a lack of pride, lack of self-esteem, you'll feel less confident and able to take stands and assert yourself.

6. *You Need the Class to Like You:* If you need your class's approval, then you will "give in" and not be able to take a stand for fear of losing their approval.

7. *You Identify with Your Students Too Much:* If you identify with the student you are trying to say "no" to, you will "feel sorry for the student" and find it difficult to uphold your standards and what you are trying to assert.

B. WORKING ON YOUR BLOCKS TO ASSERTIVENESS

1. *Guilt:* You must realize that not doing what you yourself believe in or should do, makes you guilty and, thereby, weakens your ability to assert yourself. You may get away with, e.g., not paying the money back, not doing *x*, etc., but you won't get away from *yourself* who feels guilty and weakens you at your job, your social life, your ability to relax, etc. Rectify these guilts if you want to be feel better and more assertive.

2. *Conflicting Feelings:* Discuss these feelings with yourself now. List the pros and cons; prioritize them; tell your ambivalent feelings to a friend and have the friend ask you questions to help you clarify these emotional

conflicts. Or, at least, decide your conditions for your "maybes." Then, standing on your true, clarified feelings will make you stand stronger and be more assertive.

3. *Fear of Others' Anger:* What's the worst thing this person could do to you if you really do/say what you feel? Often your fear is based on an unconscious exaggerated fantasy of the consequences, or a "transference" reaction: the other person reminds you of your father or mother; it feels like s/he will, *send you to bed without dinner.* If you feel this person will "punish" you by, e.g., leaving you, what kind of friendship is it then anyway?

4. *Fear of Your Own Anger:* You probably feel that if you let out a little anger, your whole "volcano" will blow. The solution is not to learn to control your anger; this method only builds up your anger. Instead, you need to find outlets for your irritations: exercise, aggressive play, friends who will allow you to vent, or get professional help.

5. *Low Ego:* Go out and accomplish something. Work hard on a projector or self-assignment, work on and accomplish a personal goal (do not cut corners or cheat). This will give you a sense of pride, and give you more strength to be assertive when you need to.

6. *You Need the Class to Like You:* If you had more people who liked you (friends), you would not need your students' approval so much. Go out and work on improving your friendships. Especially, try to share your tough decisions and stands that you need to take on your job with some of your colleagues and/or friends.

7. *You Identify with Your Students Too Much:* Keep in mind that that student is *not you.* Or, tell yourself that what you have to do will ultimately help the student (though it "hurts" now). You don't want to send a message to this student that manipulating and the ability to "con" the world is better than good work. Weaning your students is as important as feeding them, if you want to make them stronger for their future.

If you feel you need more help here, these books may also be helpful:

- *Your Perfect Right: A Guide to Assertive Living* by Robert E. Alberti and Michael L. Emmons, 25th anniv. edition (Atascadera, CA: Impact Publishers, October 1995).
- *Asserting Yourself: A Practical Guide for Positive Change* by Sharon Anthony Bower and Gordon H. Bower (Cambridge, MA: Da Capo Press, 2004).
- *Assertiveness at Work* by Kathleen A. Adams (Englewood Cliffs, NJ: Spectrum, 1982).

- *When I Say No I Feel Guilty* by Manuel J Smith (New York: Dial Press, 1975).

For more on assertiveness for teachers and how to curtail classroom disruptive behavior, see *Preventing Classroom Discipline Problems*, third edition, by Howard Seeman (Lanham, MD: Rowman & Littlefield Education, 1999).

Asserting yourself and taking stands is a complex and difficult skill. It warrants its own book on the subject. You can also strengthen this ability by seeing chapter 9, "Training Exercises and Checklist."

Chapter Eight

Legal Considerations

As you think about the application of some of the suggestions in the above chapters, you might find it useful to have some familiarity with legal parameters. Below are brief summaries of laws that may be relevant for you and your college. These parameters, however, change from year to year, so it is good to check (online) if you need to decide on a current issue. For college faculty: it is often best to consult your college's department/division, or your college's catalogue for what they deem legally appropriate.

For students: if they are concerned that their rights are being violated, they can consult: http://www.freechild.org/student_rights.htm where they can find the ACLU Students' Rights Directory.

Meanwhile, here are some areas that may be of concern legally:

   A. Search and Seizure
   B. Weapons in Schools
   C. Disabled Students
   D. Dress Codes
   E. Freedom of Speech
   F. Conclusions
   G. Resources

The first point to make here is that in the United States via the U.S. Constitution, each state can determine its own local education policies. Then cities of each state all come under that state's regulations. However, federal funding, and how the courts interpret the law vs. students' rights under the Constitution—have sometimes taken away or given the administrators of colleges more or less power, especially with regard to safety, which has become an overriding issue in the past few years.

A. SEARCH AND SEIZURE

The issues involved here are unfortunately in opposition to each other: students' rights to privacy vs. college administrators' needs to find ways to ensure the safety on a college campus. How much should the Fourth Amendment be invoked regarding the rights of students?

The courts have been flexible in accommodating the Fourth Amendment to the special situation presented by schools in general, where school officials have both a right and a duty to provide a safe environment conducive to education. For example, in a case that has set the standard on this issue,[1] the court noted that: against the student's interest of privacy must be set the substantial interest of teachers and administrators in maintaining discipline and safety in the classroom and on campus grounds. . . . Accordingly, we have recognized that maintaining security at a college requires a certain degree of flexibility in school disciplinary procedures. . . . These kinds of decisions have created a key criterion for search and seizures in colleges: students are entitled to protection from *unreasonable* searches and seizures. The legality of a search of a student should depend simply on the *reasonableness*, under all the circumstances of the search.[2] Considering this criterion, the following policies are probably best regarding this issue:

A. The administrators of a college should write up a search and seizure policy that spells out the criterion of the T.L.O. case regarding reasonableness. It should clearly state that the following kinds of decisions should be made in determining whether a search should be conducted:
   a. Whether a student's conduct creates a reasonable suspicion that a regulation or law has been violated.
   b. Whether the measures contemplated for the search are reasonably related to the search objectives and not excessively intrusive or harsh in light of the suspected infraction.
B. Administrators and faculty should receive in-service training regarding the school's search and seizure policy.
C. When contemplating a search of a student's person, it is always best to let a trained college security officer both make the decision about the search, and conduct the search. With regard to these searches of, e.g., belongings, or college residence, if a school administrator is going to do the search, s/he should consult with an objective third party (preferably another administrator). These professionals should discuss whether a search is *reasonable*, given the immediate situation and the methods by which the search will be conducted. All searches should be conducted by at least two faculty members of the same sex as the student being searched. The

right of the people to be secure in their persons, houses, papers, and effects against unreasonable searches and seizures, shall not be violated, and no warrant shall issue, but upon probable cause, supported by oath or affirmation, and particularly describing the place to be searched, and the persons or things to be seized.[3]

D. Notes detailing the method and nature of the search should be made during or immediately after the search. Some factors that might be considered in determining whether reasonable suspicion to search exists include:

a. the student's age, history and record in the college;
b. the prevalence and seriousness of the problem in the college to which the search was directed;
c. the exigencies in making a search without delay, and further investigation;
d. the probative value and reliability of the information used as a justification for the search;
e. the particular teacher or college official's experience with the student.

However, keep in mind that the more that law enforcement officers are involved, the more likely "probable cause" must be evident.

B. WEAPONS IN SCHOOLS

In an effort to prevent guns from being brought onto campuses, Congress enacted the "Gun-Free School Zones Act of 1990." It requires every local educational agency to have some kind of policy and procedure for the expulsion of any student (for a minimum of one year) who is determined to have brought a weapon to a school. (An exception may be made on a case-by-case basis by the chief administering officer of the school. This act has been upheld by most courts, but some cases that have invoked this act are still (1997) in appeal, mostly regarding whether the item in question should be considered a "weapon."[4]

Rep. Robert R. Damron introduced a bill in Congress (January 8, 2008) to require public colleges and universities to comply with deadly concealed weapon "carry laws." It presently has been referred to the House Judiciary Committee. One recent opinion on this issue is as follows: "The idea of allowing or even thinking about allowing guns/handguns/firearms on school property is just dumb/stupid/nuts. Remember the recent USA Supreme Court ruling only allows a person the constitutional right to own a gun in the home and home only; states and communities (colleges/schools) can still put limits and restrictions on where a person can carry a gun/firearm outside of the home, if they should be allowed to carry a gun/firearm outside of the home at all.

C. DISABLED STUDENTS

School districts should proceed carefully when contemplating discipline of a student who is deemed to have a disability. A disabled student has distinct and special rights with respect to discipline and what kinds of proceedings can be imposed (Individuals with Disabilities Education Act, 200 U.S.C., 400, et. seq.). The Supreme Court has provided a threshold standard for the administration of discipline to a student with a disability.[5]

However, the courts have found legal basis for stipulating that students with disabilities can be treated in the *same manner* as students without disabilities for *short-term* suspensions from a college and other typical disciplinary measures. For example, one can petition the court to temporarily expel a student when the individual presents a continuing threat of disruption: uses drugs or alcohol abusively on college grounds; or is carrying a weapon.[6]

D. DRESS CODES

There is an increasing body of opinion, as recognized by recent California legislation, that: "Many educators believe that school dress significantly influences student behavior." Apparel that relates to gang membership is only one instance. The courts are beginning to support educators regarding dress codes in general. For example, the courts have recently sustained rules by schools to prohibit the wearing of immodest clothing that impacts upon relationships between student and student, and student and teacher.[7]

E. FREEDOM OF SPEECH

The courts have upheld the rights of students to express their opinions, even on controversial subjects.[8] The only way to bar students of these rights is to show that the students' activities would materially and substantially disrupt the work and discipline of the college.[9]

F. CONCLUSIONS

Presently, due to some tragic events on campuses in recent years, our society is generally opting on the side of safety and violence prevention in our schools—as opposed to an overconcern for students' rights (although the

ACLU continues to fight for the latter). For example, regarding school safety and weapons in schools, schools are receiving more legal support to, e.g., curtail weapons in the courts to, hopefully, eliminate some of the more dangerous situations on campuses and in college classrooms.

G. RESOURCES

1. The Education Law Association (formerly Natl. Org. on Legal Problems of Education)
   300 College Park, Dayton, OH 45469–2280
   phone: 937-229-3589
   http://educationlaw.org/
2. The National Council on Crime Prevention
   2345 Crystal Dr., Suite 500, Arlington, VA 22202–4801
   phone: 202-466-6272
   fax: 202-296-1356
   http://www.weprevent.org
3. The National School Safety Center (NSSC)
   141 Duesenberg Dr., Suite 11, Westlake Village, CA 91362
   phone: 805-373-9977
   fax: 805-373-9277
4. National Youth Violence Prevention Resource Center http://www.safe youth.org/scripts/about/index.asp
   This is an online forum to facilitate networking and collaboration among key change agents in communities/schools, local government leaders to provide resources, training, and technical assistance to support efforts to plan, implement, and evaluate effective youth violence prevention efforts.
5. Information on freedom of speech/liberties per university is at http:// thefire.org, which defends and sustains individual rights at America's colleges and universities. These rights include freedom of speech, legal equality, due process, religious liberty, and sanctity of conscience. At this site, you can go to "Spotlight: The Campus Freedom Resource," where you can find comprehensive information on the state of liberty on America's campuses by clicking on each state on a U.S. map, and then clicking on the campus you wish information about. You can also find pages for individual academic institutions, which contain relevant links to research of speech codes, sexual harassment, case materials from FIRE's Individual Rights Defense Program, media coverage of FIRE's work, and entries from FIRE's blog, "The Torch."

NOTES

1. New Jersey v. T.L.O., 469 U.S. 325, 83 L. Ed.2d 720, 105 S. Ct. 733, 740, 1985.

2. T.L.O., 469 U.S. at 341; 105 S. Ct. at 742.

3. Horton v. Goose Creek Indep. Sch. Dist., 690 F.2d 470 (5th Cir. 1982); ruling denied, 693 F.2d 524 (5th Cir. 1982). Reed B. Day, *Legal Issues Surrounding Safe Schools,* National Organization on Legal Problems of Education, pp. 30–31.

4. Day, *Legal Issues*, p. 49.

5. Day, *Legal Issues*, p. 44.

6. ERIC NO. ED384192. Gail Sorensen, "Discipline of Students with Disabilities: An Update." (A Legal-Memorandum) National Association of Secondary School Principals, Reston, VA. June 1995.

7. Day, *Legal Issues*, p. 71.

8. Tinker v. Des Moines Indep. Comm. Sch. Dist., 393 U.S. 503, 21 L. Ed.2d 731,89 S. Ct.

9. Id., 393 U.S. at 513; 211. Ed.2d at 742.

Chapter Nine

Training Exercises and Checklist

In this chapter, there are exercises and a checklist that will help college instructors and administrators implement the concepts and skills that have been discussed in the previous chapters.

CHAPTER 2: BEING CAREFUL TO NOT MAKE MISCALLS

It is best not to mistake a "miscall" for a real "discipline problem." We must be aware to make this distinction. Some disruptions are best handled *not* with a "hammer" but with a "screwdriver."

Exercise 1

Below are all the behaviors that have been discussed in this book. Some, if handled wrongly become miscalls; while others are more clearly "discipline problems."

Place an M next to those that are Miscalls, and D next to those that are "Discipline problems" and a C = depends on certain Conditions (if C, then specify under what conditions).

Then, by looking at the item in this book's table of contents, you can see if you classified it correctly according to the explanations given in that section of this book.

Students who:

1. ____Need further instructions
2. ____Bring their young child to class
3. ____Challenge you regarding your rules
4. ____Try to manipulate you

5. ____Cheat
6. ____Blurt unreasoned answers
7. ____Sulk
8. ____Can hardly write
9. ____Are learning disabled
10. ____Ask you to repeat
11. ____Whisper during your teaching
12. ____Sleep in class
13. ____Make inappropriate demands
14. ____Argue about their lateness, absence, grades
15. ____Accuse you of racism, sexism, unfairness
16. ____Call out
17. ____Cheat
18. ____Do other homework in your class
19. ____Do not respect other students
20. ____Monopolize the discussion
21. ____Have poor personal hygiene
22. ____Text message during class
23. ____Talk while you or another student is talking
24. ____Constantly ask questions
25. ____Eat in class
26. ____Come late
27. ____Leave class early
28. ____Are withdrawn
29. ____Make constant noise
30. ____Leave class early
31. ____Use pagers, cell phones, and iPods in class
32. ____Use profanity and/or pejorative language
33. ____Are high or selling drugs
34. ____Are verbally abusive
35. ____Harass others
36. ____Plagiarize
37. ____Threaten to harm themselves or others
38. ____Are physically violent or who carry weapons

Exercise 2

Read each of the following classroom situations below, from A to Q. Then decide if is best handled as a real "Discipline problem" (D); as a "Miscall" (M); with "See me after class" (S); with the "Course Syllabus" (SY); or by using an "Engaging Teaching Method" (E).

A. ____A student comes to class late and walks to his seat by passing in front of you in front of the class.

B. ____A student puts his head down in row 4, last seat and starts to fall asleep.

C. ____Students near the back of the room keep passing notes to each other.

D. ____A student keeps looking out the window.

E. ____A student calls out for the third time.

F. ____Two students are talking to each other in the back of your class.

G. ____A student opens her book bag and everything falls on the floor and she says, "Shit!"

H. ____A student comes to class late and comes up to you while you are teaching to hand you a note about it.

I. ____While you are teaching, Carmen often turns to Jose and talks to him to explain what you said.

J. ____A student in the front of the room opens a bag of potato chips and starts to eat them.

K. ____You see John looking over the head of Mary in front of him to see her answers on a test you are giving.

L. ____A student leaves your class ten minutes early, and then does this again the next class as well.

M. ____You notice that a student is reading a magazine in your class instead of taking notes.

N. ____You call on a student who has raised her hand. She responds, "I find this stuff boring."

O. ____A student in the last seat of row 5 takes out a comb, and starts to comb her bangs to one side, and then puts the comb away.

P. ____During your lesson, you notice that a student is writing on the corners of all his notes: "This class sucks!"

Q. ____To illustrate a point, you tell the class an amusing story. At the end of it, a student raises his hand, and says, "That's not so funny!" The class laughs.

Exercise 3

Below are some typical miscalls explained in chapter 2. Which ones do you tend to fall into? Give these an X. Then re-read chapter 2 for suggestions on what to do instead of making these typical miscalls that you are prone to.

1. ____The withdrawn student
2. ____The overreacted-to rule

 3. ____The "I've got to win their feelings" need
 4. ____The "I need their attention" syndrome
 5. ____The "my ego is hurt" reaction
 6. ____"They're interfering with my getting my teaching plan done" reaction
 7. ____Displaced anger
 8. ____"I'm tired of trying to be understanding all the time" reaction.
 9. ____The mirror effect
10. ____The "I need to control" reaction
11. ____The "steam" for "smoke" mistake
12. ____The venting for cursing mistake
13. ____The prejudicial mistake
14. ____Holding a grudge
15. ____The punishing the education problem mistake

CHAPTER 3: HANDLING DISCIPLINE PROBLEMS

Exercise 4: Working on Your Lateness Policy

Picture a student coming to your class late and disturbing your teaching. What does s/he do?

_____

Now, take a look at your late policy. Handle this student by responding with your late policy here:

_____

_____

Does it handle/prevent this situation? Is this policy backed up and clearly stated in your Course Syllabus? Does your policy curtail you having to talk to this student at the beginning or during class? If it does not, revise it below so that it does.

_____

_____

_____

Exercise 5: Working on Your Absence Policy

Picture a student who was absent arguing with you about his/her absence and disturbing your teaching. What does s/he do or say?

_____

Now, take a look at your absence policy. Handle this student by responding with your absence policy here:

Does it handle/prevent this situation? Is this policy backed up and clearly stated in your Course Syllabus? Does your policy curtail you having to talk to this student at the beginning or during class? If it does not, revise it below so that it does.

Exercise 6: Working on Your Grading Policy

Picture a student who argues with you about his/her grade. What does s/he do?

Now, take a look at your grading policy. Handle this student by responding with your grading policy here:

Does it handle/prevent this situation? Is this policy backed up and clearly stated in your Course Syllabus? Does your policy curtail you having to talk to this student at the beginning or during class? If it does not, revise it below so that it does.

Exercise 7: Working on Responding to Students Who Accuse You of Racism

Picture a student accusing you of racism. What does s/he say?

Now, respond to this accusation by referring to your fair policies regarding, e.g., grades.

(Remember: you do *not* deliver this response in your class, but at, e.g., an office hour.):

Does your Course Syllabus back this up clearly? If not, note the revisions you need to make here:

_____

_____

_____

Exercise 8: Working on Responding to Students Who Accuse You of Sexism

Picture a student accusing you of sexism. What does s/he say?

_____

Now, respond to this accusation by referring to your fair policies regarding, e.g., grades.

(Remember: you do *not* deliver this response in your class, but at, e.g., an office hour.):

_____

_____

_____

Does your Course Syllabus back this up clearly? If not, note the revisions you need to make here:

_____

_____

_____

Exercise 9: Working on Responding to Students Who Accuse You of Being Unfair

Picture a student accusing you of being unfair. What does s/he say?

_____

Now, respond to this accusation by referring to your fair policies regarding, e.g., grades.

(Remember: you do *not* deliver this response midst your class, but at, e.g., an office hour.):

_____

_____

_____

Does your Course Syllabus back this up clearly? If not, note the revisions you need to make here:

_____

_____

_____

Exercise 10: Working on Your Policy Regarding Eating in Class

Picture a student eating in class in such a way that it disturbs your teaching or others' learning. What do you picture?

___

Now, respond to this situation by referring to your policy on this matter here:

___
___

Hopefully, your Course Syllabus backs this up clearly. If not, note the revisions you need to make here:

___
___

Exercise 11: Working on Responding to Students Who Are Noisy (for example, tapping a pen)

Picture a student doing that in such a way that it disturbs your teaching or others' learning. What do you picture?

___

Now, write out how you would respond:

___
___

Did you respond according to the guidelines in chapter 3?

___
___

Exercise 12: Working on Responding to Students Using a Cell Phone/iPod in Class

Picture a student taking out and using a cell phone or iPod during your class in such a way that it disturbs your teaching or others' learning. What do you picture?

___

Now, write out how you would respond:

___
___

Did you respond according to the guidelines in chapter 3?

___

Exercise 13: Working on Responding to Students Who Use Profanity

What do you picture him/her saying?

_____

Now, write out how you would respond to this:

_____

_____

_____

Did you respond according to the guidelines in chapter 3?

_____

Exercise 14: Working on Responding to Students Who Are High on a Drug

What do you picture?

_____

Now, write out how you would respond to this situation:

_____

_____

_____

Did you respond according to the guidelines in chapter 3?

_____

Exercise 15: Working on Responding to Students Who You Think Might Be Selling Drugs

What do you picture?

_____

Now, write out how you would respond to this situation:

_____

_____

_____

Did you respond according to the guidelines in chapter 3?

_____

Exercise 16: Working on Responding to Cheating

What do you picture?

_____

Now, write out how you would respond to this situation:

_____

_____

_____

Did you respond according to the guidelines in chapter 3? Is your response clearly backed up in your Course Syllabus? If not, then note the revisions that you need to make in your Course Syllabus here:

_____

_____

_____

Exercise 17: Working on Responding to Plagiarism

What typical scenario or situation do you picture?

_____

Now, write out how you would respond to this situation:

_____

_____

_____

Did you respond according to the guidelines in chapter 3? Is your response clearly backed up in your Course Syllabus? If not, then note the revisions that you need to make in your Course Syllabus here:

_____

_____

_____

Exercise 18: Working on Responding to Students Who Threaten

Imagine a student verbalizing threats. What do you picture?

_____

Now, write out how you would respond to this situation:

_____

_____

_____

Did you respond according to the guidelines in chapter 3?

_____

_____

_____

Exercise 19: Working on Responding to Physical Violence

What situation can you picture?

_____

Now, write out how you would respond to this:

_____

_____

_____

Did you respond according to the guidelines in chapter 3?

Exercise 20: Working on Responding to Students Who You Think Might Be Carrying a Weapon

What do you picture?

Now, write out how you would respond to this situation:

Did you respond according to the guidelines in chapter 3?

Exercise 21: Working on Handling/Preventing Victims of Rape

Advocate for the posting of the suggestions in chapter 3, no. 20, in your classroom and throughout your campus. Specifically:

1. The guidelines for men and women for the prevention of acquaintance rape. List them:

2. The precautionary behaviors to prevent students from becoming a victim of rape. Name some:

3. The procedures to follow after a rape has occurred, in order to successfully prosecute the offender. List them:

4. Do you know the suggestions regarding what a faculty member or administrator can do to help prevent sexual assault? Can you state at least three of these? (See chapter 3, no. 20.)

    1.

    2.

3. _____
   _____
   _____

CHAPTER 4: BEING CONGRUENT

Exercise 22: Working on Being Congruent in Your General Interaction with Your Students

Notice your demeanor and your language as you talk to your students. If they saw you in the supermarket, would you be the same person?

Review chapter 4, section C. Notice the list below: "How much of a person can I be with my students?" Which can you do (yes)? Which can you not do (no)?

- ____Joke with them sometimes.
- ____Admit some mistakes, or problems.
- ____Use your own down-to-earth words, as much as you can.
- ____Tell them sometimes how you feel about some rules and topics in the lesson.
- ____Call them by their first names.
- ____Sometimes tell them how you're feeling today as you start teaching.
- ____Pat them on the back or shoulder, if you feel it as they are near you.
- ____Don't be afraid to smile, or wave "hello" in the hall, or after school.
- ____Share a personal story (especially if it relates to the lesson).

Can you work on your ability to say *yes* more often? Can you put more of your *person* into your teacher?

Exercise 23: Working on Being Congruent Regarding Your Rules

Describe three rules/policies you try to enforce in your classroom and in your Course Syllabus.

1. _____
   _____
   _____
2. _____
   _____
   _____

3. _____
_____
_____

What are the consequences for each?

1. _____
_____
_____

2. _____
_____
_____

3. _____
_____
_____

Now give a letter grade to each of these: I believe in this (A) very much; (B) somewhat; (C) a little; (D) not at all.

1. _____
2. _____
3. _____

If you gave one a B or less, revise it so that you are more congruent with it. Revisions:

_____
_____
_____
_____

Exercise 24: Working on Congruence Regarding Your Subject Matter

List five topics you will teach this coming month.

1. _____
2. _____
3. _____
4. _____
5. _____

Now, for each, give a letter grade:

A. I think this is very important, I care about it;
B. I believe in the importance of this somewhat;
C. I don't feel this is valuable, I don't care about it;
D. I think this is useless and boring.

If you gave a topic a C or less, find more relevance for the topic, or do not teach it, or, at least, explain to the students honestly why you must go over this. For the latter ones especially, make sure you use the engagement methods in chapter 6.

CHAPTER 5: DESIGNING A COURSE SYLLABUS AS A CONTRACT

Exercise 25

Design a draft of your Course Syllabus. Now, look it over and check it that you have at least these items in it:

1. The course's catalogue number.
2. The name of the course.
3. Your name as instructor.
4. Your office hours.
5. The meeting times of the course.
6. How many credits are earned in this course.
7. A clear statement of your rules regarding certain behaviors.
8. A policy regarding cell phones, music players, etc.
9. Your grading policy regarding quizzes, tests, Exams, field work.
10. How class participation counts in the course.
11. Standards and due dates.
12. The correct format for the Final Papers.
13. The competencies or "exit requirements" for completing the course.
14. A tentative schedule of the topics that will be covered.
15. The required and supplemental reading assignments.
16. A tentative schedule of these reading assignments.
17. A tentative schedule of tests, Midterm, and Final Exam.
18. Your policies regarding: absence, lateness, leaving class early.
19. Your policy and consequences regarding cheating.
20. Your policy and consequences regarding plagiarism.

21. Your policy regarding students who need to bring their children to class.
22. Your policy regarding eating in class.

After you have checked your Course Syllabus for the above:

• Discuss your Syllabus with other instructors.
• See others' Syllabi to get ideas that are consistent with your colleagues in your department.
• Plan your first meeting of the class:
  A. How will you hand this out?

  _____

  _____

  B. How will you orally explain it to the class? (You may want to highlight the items for yourself that you want to elaborate on to the class orally.)

  _____

  _____

CHAPTER 6: METHODS TO ENGAGE THE STUDENTS

Exercise 26

Prepare a preface statement on a lecture you will give and write it out.

Try to have this statement either express how you really feel about the subject matter, or prepare a relevant personal experience you can tell the class. Make your preface talk from the "I" point of view and practice saying it personally to the student's person; say it not just from your *teacher* but from your *person* to their *person*, not just to them as *students*.

Exercise 27

Present this preface statement to either a friend or colleague and ask, Do they feel your "heart" is in it? Revise it according to their feedback here:

_____

_____

_____

Exercise 28

With a friend, explain a topic you are going to lecture on soon. Have your friend interrupt you with a "digression": e.g., "That reminds me of when I

. . ." See if you can weave this "digression" back into your lesson. Write this "weave" here:

_____

_____

_____

Or, use this "digression" to teach something relevant to what you want to get across. What will you teach? Write it out here:

_____

_____

_____

Exercise 29

Look at your plans for your next lecture. Try to figure out a way for you to ask your students to "prioritize" a list of some kind that has to do with the topic that you will teach.

_____

_____

_____

Exercise 30

Plan a role-play for the topic coming up in your next lecture. See the guidelines for this in chapter 6, no. 8. You can role-play a historic person, fictional character, or even a concept.

Exercise 31

Plan a way for the students to do a Future Projection (see chapter 6, no. 11)—where they write a letter imagining it is five or ten years from now—that can relate to what you are teaching in your coming lecture.

Exercise 32

Prepare three questions that you will ask during your next lecture.

1. _____

_____

2. _____

_____

3. _____
   _____

Now take a look at chapter 6, no. 14. Do your questions fall into the pitfalls of "bad questions" described there? Yes? Then, revise the questions here:

1. _____
   _____
2. _____
   _____
3. _____
   _____

Exercise 33

Organize a panel discussion or debate that will help students think about what you have taught. Plan it out here:

_____
_____
_____
_____
_____

Exercise 34

Take a look ahead at two coming lectures. Now, for each one create a "Felt Goal, not an Aim" for each of these lectures. See chapter 6, no. 26.

1. _____
   _____
   _____
2. _____
   _____
   _____

CHAPTER 7: WORKING ON YOUR ASSERTIVENESS

Exercise 35

Below are the "blocks" to assertiveness that weaken this ability. Place a number next to the ones that are your problem: 3—usually, 2—sometimes, 1—seldom, or 0—never.

Blocks to Assertiveness

1. ____Incongruence, thus Guilty
2. ____Inappropriateness, thus Guilty
3. ____Unfairness, thus Guilty
4. ____Guilt for Other Areas
5. ____Conflicting Feelings
6. ____Fear of Others' Anger
7. ____Fear of Your Own Anger
8. ____Low Ego
9. ____I Need the Class to Like Me
10. ____Identification with the Student(s)

Add up your score: _____.

The higher your score, the weaker you are in this ability. Ask a friend to do this exercise and compare scores. Then, share and discuss these items with him/her in order to support each other. For those areas you need work on (where you wrote a 3 or 2) reread the section of chapter 7 that relates to your weakness.

Now, redo this exercise and track your improvement:

Month	Score	I still need to:

PRACTICE: HOW WOULD YOU HANDLE
THESE SITUATIONS?

Exercise 36

Below are two classroom disruptive situations that might happen in a college classroom. Try to write out what you would do for each of these. Try to apply your new understandings and techniques from the relevant chapters of this book.

Read Situation 1. What you would do in this situation? (Then you can look down to Answer 1 to see one constructive way this situation might have been handled. Your way can be different, but hopefully effective, using your new understandings and techniques from this book.)

Situation 1

An English professor is teaching a sophomore class in American Literature. He asks the class to turn to page 123, where they find a poem by e.e. cummings, "Buffalo Bill is Defunct."

The professor starts reading the poem to the class, when a student shouts out: "Hey, this guy makes a lot of grammar errors, just like me!" The class laughs. "Maybe I deserve to be famous and get an A in this class." The class laughs again. The professor tries to maintain a sober and serious expression during these quips. The class notices no smile coming from the teacher and now others chime in with more quips: "Hey, maybe you should raise all our grades for our *poetic* grammar." The professor shouts at all of them to be quiet, and threatens some students that if they do not stop, they will . . .

Try your answer of how you would handle the above situation before you read Answer 1 below, which is only one suggested way to better handle this situation.

―――――――――――――――――――――――――――――――――――――――
―――――――――――――――――――――――――――――――――――――――
―――――――――――――――――――――――――――――――――――――――

Answer 1

The professor might have explained the differences between expository writing and poetry before presenting e.e. cummings' poetry. Also, other poets who have used correct grammar to be "poetic" might have preceded this lesson. The teacher might have laughed (since it is a cute point) and said to the student who first called out: "John: interesting point, but Cummings is not doing expository writing here. Let me explain. . . ." The teacher should only "hear" this student once he has raised his hand, and only call on hand-raisers.

Explanation

Let's face it: the student's quip was funny. This teacher's mask of not cracking a smile, hiding what was really a clever remark, only made the class want to go after the teacher more. (The teacher was not congruent.) Instead the professor might have sympathized with the students about how difficult English grammar is and that he/she also sometimes makes mistakes too.

The professor might point out why Cummings modifies the rules of grammar, e.g., to make some sentences emotionally stronger. Then, students should be allowed to write on a topic in an expository style (with correct grammar). Then, write on the same topic in poetic style, where they can revise grammar to enhance what they want to get across. The class can present both styles to the rest of the class the next day, or even sooner. This might make for a very educational lesson on poetry vs. expository writing and e.e. cummings.

Also, this teacher needs to share himself/herself as a *person* (not just as The Teacher) with the class while studying American Literature, or an authoritarian, "enemy" relationship may form with the class.

Read Situation 2. What you would do in this situation? Then look down to Answer 2 for one constructive way this situation might have been handled. Again, your way can be different, but hopefully effective, using the points in the previous chapters.

Situation 2

You are explaining something you wrote on the blackboard. In the midst of this, a student raises her hand, and you call on her: "I was late yesterday; did you mark me present?" You say: "I can't answer that now." She says, "Please look." You stop for a second and you look in your book. You say, "I marked you late, but it's the third time, so it may lower your grade." You try to go on, but she says, very annoyed: "But, I got a B+ on the last test!" You tell her, "That does not mean you will get a B+ on the Final or a B+ for the course." She gets angrier, and the whole class starts talking to their neighbors about this. Now, you start to go after those students talking to their neighbors. They also then start to get angry with you. And then things get worse.

Try your way to handle this before you read Answer 2 below, which is only one suggested way to better handle this situation.

Answer 2

This class might not have a clear Course Syllabus-contract. If the Course Syllabus specifically clarified the lateness policy, the question that the student asks might not ever have come up. Or, if the Course Syllabus is clear, you might just tell the student: "See me after class" or "at my office hour and we can discuss this" and go on. You should not look at her lateness record or handle this comment in class. After class or during your office hour, you can check her record and simply refer her to your policy in the Course Syllabus.

Explanation

These kinds of disruptive questions should have been taken care of at the first meeting of the class with a clear Course Syllabus. The teacher certainly should not have looked into this lateness during the class or threatened her with a lower grade in front of her peers. If questions and comments on lateness still persist, you should not answer her, but go on with your teaching, reminding her (with some empathy), "I understand your concern; let's discuss this later when I can respond to your concern better."

If she sulks, leaves, or just puts her head on the desk, fine. Just follow your Syllabus's contract consequences spelled out there. If she becomes disruptive, say something like: "Sue, I will help you with this lateness question later, but if you continue disrupting this class, I cannot keep teaching to prepare the class well for the midterm next week." (This will motivate some peer pressure for her to postpone her concern.)

Self-Reflection

How did you do when you compare your answers with the answer that I suggested for Situation 1?

_____

_____

How did you do when you compare your answers with the answer that I suggested for Situation 2?

_____

What do you tend to do well?

_____

_____

What do you NOT do well, or, need to be careful that you don't do . . . ?

What do you need to make sure you DO?

Do you have some knee-jerk reactions to some situations that are NOT the best way to respond?

What reactions do you need to re-train in yourself and practice?

What chapters should you review and work on in this book?

CHECKLIST

Before you start each semester, check these reminders.

1. Are you inappropriately losing your patience with: "the well-to-do," "the immature," or "the learning disabled" students? (Chapter 2)
2. Can you distinguish the manipulators ("the game players") from others, such as "the immature"? (Chapter 2)
3. Are you making miscalls? (Chapter 2)
4. Have you set aside some "late chairs" near the entrance door to your class? (Chapter 2)
5. Do you know the how/where to refer students to the facility at your college that can help students with writing difficulties? (Chapter 2)
6. Do you know the how/where to refer students to the facility at your college that can help students with disabilities? (Chapter 2)

7. Is your course syllabus clear, detailed enough, and congruent for you? (Chapter 5)

8. Are you following through with what you said in your Course Syllabus about absence? (Chapters 4 and 5)

9. Are you following through with what you said in your Course Syllabus about lateness? (Chapters 4 and 5)

10. Are you following through with what you said in your Course Syllabus about leaving class early? (Chapters 4 and 5)

11. Are you following through with what you said in your Course Syllabus about cheating? (Chapters 4 and 5)

12. Are you following through with what you said in your Course Syllabus about plagiarism? (Chapters 4 and 5)

13. Are you following through with what you said in your Course Syllabus about bringing children to class? (Chapters 4 and 5)

14. Are you following through with what you said in your Course Syllabus about eating in class? (Chapters 4 and 5)

15. Are you using enough methods in your lectures to engage the students? (Chapter 6)

16. Are you having any prejudicial feelings that you need to correct? (Chapter 2)

17. Have you prepared your first class meeting: What you will say to them, how you will go over your Course Syllabus? (Chapter 5)

18. Have you decided what your specific warning steps will be if a student does not heed your policies? (Chapter 5)

19. Are you nervous about taking a stand or asserting yourself regarding the standards that you have set forth in you Course Syllabus? (Chapters 5 and 7)

20. Are you feeling guilty about anything that may sap your assertiveness? (Chapter 7)

21. Do you need to work on some ambivalences you feel that you hope to implement in your Course Syllabus? (Chapter 7)

22. Are you feeling a bit lonely on and outside your job, such that you worry about the students' approval too much—and thereby not uphold your standards, or be susceptible to their manipulations? (Chapter 7)

23. Are you feeling a general lack of confidence? Do you need to prepare your lectures better before you teach each day? (Chapter 6)

24. Have you posted prominently the help phone numbers for students to report/get help for sexual assaults? (Chapter 3, no. 20)

25. Have you posted prominently your college's emergency phone numbers for getting help with, e.g., binge drinking, noticing weapons on campus?

Or, have you at least posted the national hotline phone number for Campus Security, (888-251-7959)? (Chapter **3**)

For more exercises and checklists to curtail disruptive behavior, see Howard Seeman's *Preventing Classroom Discipline Problems*, third edition (Lanham, MD: Rowman & Littlefield Education, 2000).

Part Three

THIS BOOK AS A HANDBOOK

Appendix A:
Index of Disruptive Behaviors
and Their Solutions

Below is an alphabetical list of disruptive behaviors and the pages where the reader can find information about preventing and handling them.

Appendix B: Questionnaire for Deans, Chairs, and Professors: Assessing Frequency/Kinds of Disruptive Behaviors

If you are a chair of a department or dean of a division, you may want to ask your faculty to fill out this assessment questionnaire and return it anonymously. Then, you can help your entire staff with the suggestions in this book by giving the book to the appropriate faculty.

If you are a college instructor/professor, you may find it helpful to keep track of the disruptive behaviors that you have had in your classrooms. You may not be alone with experiencing these. You can then share this information with your colleagues, either formally or informally. Often just noticing these behaviors and their frequency can lead to very constructive conversations and changes (as suggested by this book) that can improve the performance of your whole department.

ASSESSMENT OF DISRUPTIVE BEHAVIORS

Please return this to my mailbox by _____. No need to identify yourself. This will be kept confidential. I hope that the information gathered here will help us all prevent and curtail disruptive behaviors in our classes.

Thank you.

I hereby report the following disruptive behaviors for the semester: _____,
year: _____.
In my course/section: _____(optional)
Today's date: _____

Problem Frequency: o=often, s=sometimes, n=never
____Absence
____Accusing you of being unfair
____Accusing you of racism
____Accusing you of sexism
____Alibis
____Arguing
____Being high on drugs in class
____Bring children to class
____Brown-nosing
____Calling out
____Carrying weapons
____Cell phones
____Challenging you
____Cheating
____Constant questions
____Cursing
____Dissing other students
____Doing other work in class
____Drug abuse
____Eating in class
____Excuses
____Fighting
____Grading arguments
____Harassment
____Inappropriate demands
____Interrupting you
____Intoxication
____iPods
____Lateness

____Leaving class early
____Manipulating
____Missing homework
____Monopolizing the discussion
____Not paying attention
____Physical violence
____Plagiarism
____Poor attendance
____Poor personal hygiene (e.g., offensive body odor)
____Profanity
____Racism
____Rape
____Sexual assaults
____Selling drugs
____Sleeping in class
____Snoring
____Talking when you're teaching
____Tapping pencils/pens
____Text-messaging
____Threats
____Verbal abuse
____Carrying weapons
____Whispering
____Withdrawn students
____Other: _____
____Other: _____
____Other: _____

Appendix C: Free Online Consultation with the Author

You can contact:
Howard Seeman, Ph.D., Professor Emeritus at
www.ClassroomManagementOnline.com
for

- Specific Help with Your Problems
- Workshops/Talks at Your College
- Questions?

All discussions are conducted with total confidentiality—just mention that you have this book.

About the Author

Howard Seeman, Ph.D., The New School for Social Research, Professor Emeritus, City University of New York, taught educational psychology and supervised teachers and evaluated professors at all levels of college teacher education at a four-year institution mainly of minority students from economically deprived areas of New York City since 1970. He has taught and consulted nationally on classroom management and preventing/handling classroom disruptive behavior since 1973.

His book, *Preventing Classroom Discipline Problems; A Classroom Management Handbook, K-12* is now in its third edition, with its own training Video/CD. It is used in over 400 school districts coast to coast in the United States and internationally in more than thirty-five countries. He has been the keynote speaker at many state/national education conferences, published over twenty articles in professional journals on education, counseling, philosophy, and psychology, and has been a major contributor to online education publications. He has also been interviewed on various radio-talk shows and has conducted over sixty workshops throughout the United States on classroom management, prevention of disruptive behavior, and emotional education. Dr. Seeman was also a visiting professor in Japan from 1990 to 1992. He holds *Certification for Training in School Violence Prevention and Intervention.*

Prior to his work above, Dr. Seeman was a camp director for ten years, co-directed a camp for emotionally disturbed children, worked in children's shelters, and taught in the New York City public schools as a licensed substitute teacher, and full-time High School English and Social Studies teacher. Prof. Seeman also teaches an online course, "Preventing Discipline Problems and Classroom Management" at www.ClassroomManagementOnline.com, where readers may contact him for further consultation, as well as find info on having workshops and talks at their college.